The Poems and Prayers of
Helen Steiner Rice

Other books featuring Helen Steiner Rice and her work

An Instrument of Your Peace
Awake My Soul and Sing: Poems Inspired by Favorite Hymns
Celebrations of the Heart
God's Promises from A to Z
The Just Because Series
       Moments of Celebration
       Moments of Comfort
       Moments of Friendship
       Moments of Love
Mother, I Love You

The Poems and Prayers of
Helen Steiner Rice

COMPILED BY VIRGINIA J. RUEHLMANN

A CROSSINGS BOOK CLUB EXCLUSIVE,
CREATED IN PARTNERSHIP WITH

Fleming H. Revell
A Division of Baker Book House Co
Grand Rapids, Michigan 49516

Published by Fleming H. Revell
a division of Baker Book House Company
P.O. Box 6287, Grand Rapids, MI 49516-6287

Printed in the United States of America

ISBN 0-7394-3696-1

A HELEN STEINER RICE™ Product created for Crossings Book Club

Cover Portrait: Glen Tracy on April 2, 1933, when Helen was 32 years old.

Helen Steiner at age 27 in 1927.

Contents

Foreword

Helen Steiner Rice could not have imagined when she began pouring her faith out in verse that God would transcribe her work into hearts throughout our nation and world. Yet she seemed to speak for us in our greatest losses and our grandest celebrations. Her words captured our pulse and comforted our grief. Even with the test of time, her writings, like a harbinger of spring, continue to bring cheer. Only someone who has known the devastation of loss and the grandeur of hope could write with such poignancy, relevancy, and beauty.

To say that Helen Steiner Rice was prolific would be to underestimate her offerings. She was more than just a regular contributor for books and cards; she was a deep well of inspiration and a refreshing spring of God's love. Her work is not just about rhyming words, but also about phrases spun in harmony with truth, which is why they so easily fit inside of us.

Yes, Helen Steiner Rice could never have imagined how God would use her broken heart and her steady faith to leave footprints of grace for us to trace.

If your life is as frenetic as mine, prepare to find rest for your racing pulse and pleasure for your crowded mind as we enter into a storehouse of melodic consolation.

Patsy Clairmont,
Women of Faith speaker
Author of *The Hat Box* and *The Shoe Box*

Introduction

Perhaps you have a favorite Helen Steiner Rice poem. I do. Maybe you found it on a greeting card or in a book of verses sent by a friend at a time of turmoil. My favorite starts with the words, "Take me and break me and make me, dear God, just what You want me to be." Like a song whose tune replays in my mind, the lines of that poem come to me automatically when I am under stress. For many people, the inspirational words of Helen Steiner Rice are like that. They come to mind unbidden at the exact right moment. Today, as during her lifetime, Helen always seems to have the right words for any occasion.

Perhaps that is because Helen herself lived so fully. To write authentically, as she did, about so many of life's ordinary and extraordinary moments, she had to have experienced them. When she addressed life's losses in her poetry, she was drawing from the wellsprings of her own losses—the untimely death of her father when she was only eighteen and the suicide of her husband during the Great Depression. When she resonated with the joy that comes from genuine family love and true friendship, she was tapping her deep emotional bonds with her mother and sister, her friends and, eventually, her readers and correspondents. And when she seemed to understand precisely how relationship with God cycles through good times and trials, she was describing her own relationship with God that had been tested and refined, stretched and strengthened, over many years.

As much as we resonate with the accuracy of Helen's verses, they tell only part of the story of this woman of many dimensions. Helen's business acumen, even at the age of twenty, startled her employers at the Lorain Electric Light and Power Company, where she catapulted from window dresser to advertising executive almost overnight. Her determination to live joyfully and graciously touched the lives of her coworkers at Gibson Greetings, and the archives at the Helen Steiner Rice Foundation bear witness to the fact that she took note of the births of their children, their wedding anniversaries, their illnesses and retirements, often by writing them personalized poems. Helen loved the quiet of the backyard at her simple family home in Lorain, Ohio, and she savored the excitement of book signings designed to promote her writing to the public. She sought the solitude of her small apartment at the Gibson Hotel in Cincinnati and reveled in the companionship of friends over chow mein at Wong's Chinese Restaurant. While she preferred to be pleasant, she was not afraid to speak her mind, something the Internal Revenue Service learned when they questioned her charitable giving!

Above all, however, Helen Steiner Rice lived in congruence with the Christian beliefs that formed the underpinnings of so many of her poems. She tithed at two churches, supported many charities, gave scholarships to needy students, and wrote compassionate letters—even as she was suffering from physical disabilities herself—to those who were broken by life. Long before the phrase "faith-based initiative" had moved into popular vocabulary, the faith-based initiative of Helen Steiner Rice found expression in her professional standards, her business ethics, her personal life, and, of course, her inspiring and well-loved poetry.

Reading this volume is like looking through a kaleidoscope. A different view of Helen Steiner Rice appears with the turn of each page. Virginia J. Ruehlmann has spent more than twenty years gathering into dozens of volumes the verses that reveal Helen's energy, enthusiasm, and love of life. This extensive collection draws on Virginia Ruehlmann's finely tuned sensitivity to all that Helen represents. It will surely be a source of delight to those who have long enjoyed the work of America's unofficial poet laureate of inspirational verse and to those who are just being introduced to her as well.

Virginia Wiltse,
Helen Steiner Rice biographer
with Ronald Pollitt
of *Helen Steiner Rice: Ambassador of Sunshine*

Beauty of
Earth and
Nature

The Heavens Declare the Glory of God

You ask me how I know it's true that there is a living God.
A God who rules the universe—the sky, the sea, the sod—
A God who holds all creatures in the hollow of His hand,
A God who put infinity in one tiny grain of sand,
A God who made the seasons—winter, summer, fall and spring—
And put His flawless rhythm into each created thing,
A God who hangs the sun out slowly with the break of day
And gently takes the stars in and puts the night away,
A God whose mighty handiwork defies the skill of man,
For no architect can alter God's perfect master plan.
What better answers are there to prove His holy being
Than the wonders all around us that are ours just for the seeing.

Fulfillment

Apple blossoms bursting wide
   now beautify the tree
And make a springtime picture
   that is beautiful to see.
Oh fragrant, lovely blossoms,
   you'll make a bright bouquet
If I but break your branches
   from the apple tree today,
But if I break your branches
   and make your beauty mine,
You'll bear no fruit in season
   when severed from the vine,
And when we cut ourselves away
   from guidance that's divine,

Our lives will be as fruitless
    as the branch without the vine.
For as the flowering branches
    depend upon the tree
To nourish and fulfill them
    till they reach futurity,
We too must be dependent
    on our Father up above,
For we are but the branches,
    and He's the tree of love.

This Is My Father's World

Everywhere across the land
You see God's face and touch His hand
Each time you look up in the sky
Or watch the fluffy clouds drift by,
Or feel the sunshine, warm and bright,
Or watch the dark night turn to light,
Or hear a bluebird brightly sing,
Or see the winter turn to spring,
Or stop to pick a daffodil,
Or gather violets on some hill,
Or touch a leaf or see a tree,
It's all God whispering, "This is Me . . .
And I am faith and I am light
And in Me there shall be no night."

The Masterpiece

Framed by the vast, unlimited sky,
Bordered by mighty waters,
Sheltered by beautiful woodland groves,
Scented with flowers that bloom and die,
    Protected by giant mountain peaks
    The land of the great unknown
    Snowcapped and towering, a nameless place
    That beckons man on as the gold he seeks,
Bubbling with life and earthly joys,
Reeking with pain and mortal strife,
Dotted with wealth and material gains
Built on ideals of girls and boys,
    Streaked with toil, opportunity's banner unfurled
    Stands out the masterpiece of art
    Painted by the one great God
    A picture of the world.

The Soul, like Nature, Has Seasons, Too

When you feel cast down and despondently sad
And you long to be happy and carefree and glad,
Do you ask yourself, as I so often do,
Why must there be days that are cheerless and blue?
Why is the song silenced in the heart that was gay?
And then I ask God what makes life this way,
And His explanation makes everything clear—
The soul has its seasons the same as the year.
Man too must pass through life's autumn of death
And have his heart frozen by winter's cold breath,
But spring always comes with new life and birth,
Followed by summer to warm the soft earth . . .

And oh, what a comfort to know there are reasons
That souls, like nature, must too have their seasons—
Bounteous seasons and barren ones, too,
Times for rejoicing and times to be blue . . .
For with nothing but sameness how dull life would be,
For only life's challenge can set the soul free . . .
And it takes a mixture of both bitter and sweet
To season our lives and make them complete.

There's Always a Springtime

After the winter comes the spring
    to show us again that in everything
There's always a renewal divinely planned,
    flawlessly perfect, the work of God's hand.
And just like the seasons that come and go
    when the flowers of spring lay buried in snow,
God sends to the heart in its winter of sadness
    a springtime awakening of new hope and gladness,
And loved ones who sleep in a season of death
    will, too, be awakened by God's life-giving breath.

April

April comes with cheeks a-glowing,
Silver streams are all a-flowing,
Flowers open wide their eyes
In lovely rapturous surprise.
Lilies dream beside the brooks,
Violets in meadow nooks,
And the birds gone wild with glee
Fill the woods with melody.

Spring Song

"The earth is the Lord's and the fullness thereof"—
It speaks of His greatness and it sings of His love,
And the wonder and glory of the first Easter morn,
Like the first Christmas night when the Savior was born,
Are blended together in symphonic splendor
And God, with a voice that is gentle and tender,
Speaks to all hearts attuned to His voice,
Bidding His listeners to gladly rejoice.
For He who was born to be crucified
Arose from the grave to be glorified.
And the birds in the trees and the flowers of spring
All join in proclaiming this heavenly King.

A Time of Many Miracles

Flowers sleeping 'neath the snow,
Awakening when the spring winds blow,
Leafless trees so bare before
Gowned in lacy green once more,
Hard, unyielding, frozen sod
Now softly carpeted by God,
Still streams melting in the spring
Rippling over rocks that sing,
Barren, windswept, lonely hills
Turning gold with daffodils—
These miracles are all around
Within our sight and touch and sound,
As true and wonderful today
As when the stone was rolled away,
Proclaiming to all doubting men
That in God all things live again.

The Beauty of Spring

God lives in the beauty
    that comes with spring—
The colorful flowers,
    the birds that sing—
And He lives in people
    as kind as you,
And He lives in all
    the nice things you do.

Little Springtime Prayer

God, grant this little springtime prayer
And make our hearts, grown cold with care,
Once more aware of the waking earth
Now pregnant with life and bursting with birth . . .
For how can man feel any fear or doubt
When on every side all around and about
The March winds blow across man's face
And whisper of God's power and grace?
Oh, give us faith to believe again
That peace on earth, good will to men
Will follow this winter of man's mind
And awaken his heart and make him kind . . .
And just as great nature sends the spring
To give new birth to each sleeping thing,
God, grant rebirth to man's slumbering soul
And help him forsake his selfish goal.

After the Winter God Sends the Spring

Springtime is a season
　of hope and joy and cheer—
There's beauty all around us
　to see and touch and hear . . .
So no matter how downhearted
　and discouraged we may be,
New hope is born when we behold
　leaves budding on a tree
Or when we see a timid flower
　push through the frozen sod
And open wide in glad surprise
　its petaled eyes to God . . .
For this is just God saying,
　"Lift up your eyes to Me,
And the bleakness of your spirit,
　like the budding springtime tree,
Will lose its wintry darkness
　and your heavy heart will sing."
For God never sends the winter
　without the joy of spring.

Spring Awakens What Autumn Puts to Sleep

A garden of asters in varying hues,
Crimson pinks and violet blues,
Blossoming in the hazy fall,
Wrapped in autumn's lazy pall . . .
But early frost stole in one night,
And like a chilling, killing blight
It touched each pretty aster's head,
And now the garden's still and dead,
And all the lovely flowers that bloomed
Will soon be buried and entombed

In winter's icy shroud of snow . . .
But oh, how wonderful to know
That after winter comes the spring
To breathe new life in everything,
And all the flowers that fell in death
Will be awakened by spring's breath . . .
For in God's plan both men and flowers
Can only reach bright, shining hours
By dying first to rise in glory
And prove again the Easter story.

The Mystery and Miracle of His Creative Hand

In the beauty of a snowflake
    falling softly on the land
Is the mystery and the miracle
    of God's great, creative hand.
What better answers are there
    to prove His holy being
Than the wonders all around us
    that are ours just for the seeing?

My Garden of Prayer

My garden beautifies my yard
    and adds fragrance to the air,
But it is also my cathedral
    and my quiet place of prayer.
So little do we realize
    that the glory and the power
Of Him who made the universe
    lies hidden in a flower!

Finding Faith in a Flower

Sometimes when faith is running low
And I cannot fathom why things are so,
I walk among the flowers that grow
And learn the answers to all I would know . . .
For among my flowers I have come to see
Life's miracle and its mystery,
And standing in silence and reverie,
My faith comes flooding back to me.

I Come to Meet You

I come to meet You, God, and as I linger here
I seem to feel You very near.
A rustling leaf, a rolling slope
Speak to my heart of endless hope.
The sun just rising in the sky,
The waking birdlings as they fly,
The grass all wet with morning dew
Are telling me I just met You . . .
And, gently, thus the day is born
As night gives way to breaking morn,
And once again I've met You, God,
And worshipped on Your holy sod . . .
For who could see the dawn break through
Without a glimpse of heaven and You?
For who but God could make the day
And softly put the night away?

Family

To My Sister

If I knew the place where wishes come true,
That's where I would go for my wish for you,
And I'd wish you all that you're wishing for,
For no sister on earth deserves it more . . .
But trials and troubles come to us all,
For that's the way we grow heaven-tall . . .
And my birthday prayer to our Father above
Is to keep you safe in His infinite love,
And we both know that gifts don't mean much
Compared to our love and God's blessed touch.

New Blessings

And now you are Mrs. instead of Miss,
And you've sealed your wedding vows with a kiss.
Your future lies in your hands, my dear,
For it's yours to mold from year to year.
God grant that you make it a beautiful thing,
With all of the blessings that marriage can bring.
May you and that fine, lucky man of your choice
Find daily new blessings to make you rejoice,
And year after year may you go on together
Always finding a rainbow regardless of weather . . .
And when youthful charms have faded away,
May you look back with joy to your glad wedding day
And thank God for helping to make you a wife
Who discovered the blessings of a full married life.

To My Husband

In my eyes there lies no vision
But the sight of your dear face.
In my heart there is no feeling
But the warmth of your embrace.
In my mind there are no thoughts
But the thoughts of you, my dear.
In my soul no other longing
But just to have you near.
All my dreams were built around you
And I've come to know it's true,
In my life there is no living
That is not a part of you.

What Is Marriage?

It is sharing and caring,
   giving and forgiving,
   loving and being loved,
   walking hand in hand,
   talking heart to heart,
   seeing through each other's eyes,
   laughing together,
   weeping together,
   praying together,
   and always trusting and believing
   and thanking God for each other . . .
For love that is shared is a beautiful thing—
It enriches the soul and makes the heart sing.

The Miracle of a Marriage

Marriage is the union of two people in love,
And love is sheer magic, for it's woven of
Gossamer dreams, enchantingly real,
That people in love are privileged to feel . . .
But the exquisite ecstasy that captures the heart
Of two people in love is just a small part
Of the beauty and wonder and miracle of
That growth and fulfillment and evolvement of love . . .
For only long years of living together
And caring and sharing in all kinds of weather
Both pleasure and pain, the glad and the sad,
Teardrops and laughter, the good and the bad
Can add new dimensions and lift love above
The rapturous ecstasies of falling in love . . .
For ecstasy passes, but it is replaced
By something much greater that cannot be defaced,
For what was in part has now become whole,
For on the wings of the flesh, love entered the soul.

With God as Your Partner

It takes a groom, it takes a bride—
Two people standing side by side.
It takes a ring and vows that say
This is our happy wedding day . . .
But wedding vows are sanctified
And loving hearts are unified
When, standing with the bride and groom,
Unseen by others in the room,
The spirit of the Lord is there
To bless this happy bridal pair . . .
For God is love, and married life
Is richer for both man and wife

When God becomes a partner, too,
In everything they plan and do . . .
And every home is specially blessed
When God is made a daily guest . . .
For married folks who pray together
Are happy folks who stay together,
For when God's love becomes a part
Of body, mind, and soul and heart,
Their love becomes a wondrous blending
That's both eternal and unending—
And God looks down and says, "Well done,"
For now you two are truly one.

Remember These Words

We are gathered together on this happy day
To stand before God and to reverently say,
"I take thee to be my partner for life,
To love with and live with as husband and wife,
To have and to hold forever, sweetheart,
Through sickness and health, until death do us part,
To love and to cherish whatever betide,
And in better or worse to stand by your side."
We do not take this lightly, but solemnly, Lord,
Asking Thy blessing as we live in accord
With Thy holy precepts, which join us in love
And assure us Thy guidance and grace from above . . .
And grant us, dear Lord, that "I will" and "I do"
Are words that grow deeper and more meaningful, too,
Through long, happy years of caring and sharing,
Secure in the knowledge that we are preparing
A love that is endless and never can die
But finds its fulfillment with You in the sky.

When Two People Marry

Your hearts are filled with happiness
　so great and overflowing
You cannot comprehend it,
　for it's far beyond all knowing
How any heart could hold such joy
　or feel the fullness of
The wonder and the glory
　and the ecstasy of love.
You wish that you could capture it
　and never let it go
So you might walk forever
　in its magic, radiant glow,
But love in all its ecstasy
　is such a fragile thing,
Like gossamer in cloudless skies
　or a hummingbird's small wing . . .
But love that lasts forever
　must be made of something strong—
The kind of strength that's gathered
　when the heart can hear no song.
When the sunshine of your wedding day
　runs into stormy weather,
And hand in hand you brave the gale
　and climb steep hills together,
And, clinging to each other
　while the thunder rolls above,
You seek divine protection
　in faith and hope and love . . .
For days of wine and roses
　never make love's dreams come true—
It takes sacrifice and teardrops
　and problems shared by two
To give true love its beauty,
　its grandeur and its fineness,
And to mold an earthly ecstasy
　into heavenly divineness.

Heart Throbs for the Man I Married

Don't think because I'm married
That all romance is dead.
Why, I'm as full of sentiment
As the day that I was wed.
Life surely would be very dull
Without a love affair.
I have to have someone around
For whom I really care.
My heart's still doing flip-flops
And beating double time.
It's full of many happy thoughts
For a dear sweetheart of mine.
And on this day of romance
I send a loving dart
From the little bow of Cupid
To pierce my lover's heart.
And believe me there's no Valentine
That carries love more true
Than the one I send my sweetheart,
Who is the man I'm married to!

With Faith in Each Other—And Faith in the Lord

With faith in each other
    and faith in the Lord
May your marriage be blessed
    with love's priceless reward,
For love that endures
    and makes life worth living
Is built on strong faith
    and unselfish giving . . .
So have faith, and the Lord
    will guide both of you through
The glorious new life
    that is waiting for you.

Remembrance Road

There's a road I call remembrance
    where I walk each day with you.
It's a pleasant, happy road, my dear,
    all filled with memories true.
Today it leads me through a spot
    where I can dream awhile,
And in its tranquil peacefulness
    I touch your hand and smile.
There are hills and fields and budding trees
    and stillness that's so sweet
That it seems that this must be the place
    where God and humans meet.
I hope we can go back again
    and golden hours renew,
And God go with you always, dear,
    until the day we do.

Motherhood

The dearest gifts that heaven holds,
    the very finest, too,
Were made into one pattern
    that was perfect, sweet, and true.
The angels smiled, well pleased, and said,
    "Compared to all the others,
This pattern is so wonderful
    let's use it just for mothers!"
And through the years, a mother
    has been all that's sweet and good,
For there's a bit of God and love
    in all true motherhood.

What Is a Mother?

It takes a mother's love
   to make a house a home—
A place to be remembered
   no matter where we roam.
It takes a mother's patience
   to bring a child up right
And her courage and her cheerfulness
   to make a dark day bright.
It takes a mother's thoughtfulness
   to mend the heart's deep hurts
And her skill and her endurance
   to mend little socks and shirts.
It takes a mother's kindness
   to forgive us when we err,
To sympathize in trouble
   and to bow her head in prayer.
It takes a mother's wisdom
   to recognize our needs
And to give us reassurance
   by her loving words and deeds.

Mothers Were Once Daughters

Every home should have a daughter,
    for there's nothing like a girl
To keep the world around her
    in one continuous whirl.
From the moment she arrives on earth
    and on through womanhood,
A daughter is a female
    who is seldom understood.
One minute she is laughing,
    the next she starts to cry—
Man just can't understand her
    and there's just no use to try.
She is soft and sweet and cuddly
    but she's also wise and smart—
She's a wondrous combination
    of mind and brain and heart . . .
And even in her baby days
    she's just a born coquette,
And anything she really wants
    she manages to get,
For even at a tender age
    she uses all her wiles,
And she can melt the hardest heart
    with the sunshine of her smiles . . .
She starts out as a rosebud,
    with her beauty unrevealed,
Then through a happy childhood
    her petals are unsealed.
She's soon a sweet girl graduate
    and then a blushing bride
And then a lovely woman
    as the rosebud opens wide . . .

And someday in the future,
    if it be God's gracious will,
She too will be a mother
    and know that reverent thrill
That comes to every mother
    whose heart is filled with love
When she beholds the angel
    that God sent her from above . . .
And there would be no life at all
    in this world or the other
Without a darling daughter
    who in turn becomes a mother.

Life's Fairest Flower

I have a garden within my soul of marvelous beauty rare,
Wherein the blossoms of all my life bloom ever in splendor fair.
Amid all this beauty and splendor, one flower stands forth as queen
Alone in its great dazzling beauty, alone but ever supreme.
The flower of love and devotion has guided me all through my life;
Softening my grief and my trouble, sharing my toil and strife.
This flower has helped me conquer temptation so black and grim,
And led me to victory and honor over my enemy, Sin.
I have vainly sought in my garden thru blossoms of love and light—
For a flower of equal wonder, to compare with this one so bright.
But ever I met with failure, my search has been in vain—
For never a flower existed, like the blossom I can claim.
For after years I now can see, amid life's roses and rue—
God's greatest gift to a little child, my darling Mother, was you.

This poem was written when Helen E. Steiner was eighteen years old.

Mother Is a Word Called Love

Mother is a word called love,
And all the world is mindful of
That the love that's given and shown to others
Is different from the love of mothers . . .
For mothers play the leading roles
In giving birth to little souls—
For though small souls are heaven-sent
And we realize they're only lent,
It takes a mother's loving hands
And her gentle heart that understands
To mold and shape this little life
And shelter it from storm and strife . . .
No other love than mother love
Could do the things required of
The one to whom God gives the keeping
Of His wee lambs, awake or sleeping . . .
So mothers are a special race
God sent to earth to take His place,
And "Mother" is a lovely name
That even saints are proud to claim.

Mothers Are Special People

Mothers are special people
In a million different ways,
And merit loving compliments
And many words of praise,
For a mother's aspiration
Is for her family's success,
To make the family proud of her
And bring them happiness . . .
And like our heavenly Father,
She's a patient, loving guide,
Someone we can count on
To be always on our side.

A Mother's Love

A mother's love is something
    that no one can explain—
It is made of deep devotion
    and of sacrifice and pain.
It is endless and unselfish
    and enduring, come what may,
For nothing can destroy it
    or take that love away.
It is patient and forgiving
    when all others are forsaking,
And it never fails or falters
    even though the heart is breaking.
It believes beyond believing
    when the world around condemns,
And it glows with all the beauty
    of the rarest, brightest gems.
It is far beyond defining,
    it defies all explanation,
And it still remains a secret
    like the mysteries of creation—
A many-splendored miracle
    man cannot understand
And another wondrous evidence
    of God's tender, guiding hand.

The Greatest Career

So glad a tiny baby came
To share your life and love and name,
For no doubt she is the greatest claim
That you have ever had to fame . . .
And don't misunderstand me, dear,
You were a star in your career,
But what, I ask you, is success
Compared with heaven's happiness?
And how could plaudits anywhere
Be half as wonderful and fair?
For this experience of the heart
Surpasses any skill or art,
For man excels in every line
But woman has a gift divine,
And in this world there is no other
As greatly honored as a mother.

It's So Nice to Have a Dad around the House

Dads are special people
    no home should be without,
For every family will agree
    they're so nice to have about . . .
They are a happy mixture
    of a small boy and a man,
And they're very necessary
    in every family plan . . .
Sometimes they're most demanding
    and stern and firm and tough,
But underneath they're soft as silk,
    for this is just a bluff . . .
But in any kind of trouble
    Dad reaches out his hand,
And you can always count on him
    to help and understand . . .

And while we do not praise Dad
　　as often as we should,
We love him and admire him,
　　and, while that's understood,
It's only fair to emphasize
　　his importance and his worth,
For if there were no loving dads,
　　this would be a loveless earth.

A Gift of Life

A baby is a gift of life
　　born of the wonder of love—
A little bit of eternity
　　sent from the Father above,
Giving a new dimension
　　to the love between husband and wife
And putting an added new meaning
　　to the wonder and mystery of life.

Baby

A wee bit of heaven
　　drifted down from above—
A handful of happiness,
　　a heart full of love.
The mystery of life
　　so sacred and sweet,
The giver of joy
　　so deep and complete.
Precious and priceless,
　　so lovable, too—
The world's sweetest miracle,
　　baby, is you.

Hush-a-Bye, Honey

Hush-a-bye, hush-a-bye, my sleepy head,
Angels are waiting to tuck you in bed.
Go to sleep, go to sleep, close your bright eyes,
Night time is tumbling out of the skies.
Angels are waiting their vigil to keep,
The sandman is filling your wee eyes with sleep.
Hush-a-bye, Baby, hush-a-bye, Sweet,
Playtime is over for tired, tiny feet.
Close your eyes, Honey, sleepy time's here,
Good-night, Little Darling, Good-night, Little Dear.

Friends

Everyone Needs Someone

Everybody everywhere, no matter what his station,
Has moments of deep loneliness and quiet desperation,
For this lost and lonely feeling is inherent in mankind,
It is just the spirit speaking as God tries again to find
An opening in the wall man builds against God's touch,
For he feels so sufficient that he doesn't need God much,
So he vainly goes on struggling to find some explanation
For these disturbing, lonely moods of inner isolation,
But the answer keeps eluding him, for in his finite mind,
He does not even recognize that he will never find
The reason for life's emptiness unless he learns to share
The problems and burdens that surround him everywhere,
But when his eyes are opened and he really looks at others,
He begins to see not strangers but people who are brothers.
So open up your hardened hearts and let God enter in,
He only wants to help you a new life to begin,
And every day's a good day to lose yourself in others,
And any time's a good time to see mankind as brothers,
And this can only happen when you realize it's true
That everyone needs someone and that "someone" is you.

Strangers Are Friends We Haven't Met Yet

God knows no strangers, He loves us all,
The poor, the rich, the great, the small.
He is a Friend who is always there
To share our troubles and lessen our care.
For no one is a stranger in God's sight,
For God is love, and in His light
May we too try in our small way
To make new friends from day to day.
So pass no stranger with an unseeing eye,
For God may be sending a new friend by.

A Friend Is a Gift from God

Among the great and glorious gifts
    our heavenly Father sends
Is the gift of understanding
    that we find in loving friends . . .
For in this world of trouble
    that is filled with anxious care,
Everybody needs a friend
    in whom they're free to share
The little secret heartaches
    that lay heavy on the mind—
Not just a mere acquaintance,
    but someone who's just our kind . . .
For somehow in the generous heart
    of loving, faithful friends,
The good God in His charity
    and wisdom always sends
A sense of understanding
    and the power of perception
And mixes these fine qualities
    with kindness and affection . . .
So when we need some sympathy
    or a friendly hand to touch
Or one who listens
    and speaks words that mean so much,
We seek a true and trusted friend
    in the knowledge that we'll find
A heart that's sympathetic
    and an understanding mind . . .
And often just without a word
    there seems to be a union
Of thoughts and kindred feelings,
    for God gives true friends communion.

Happiness

Across the years, we've met in dreams
And shared each other's hopes and schemes.
We've known a friendship rich and rare
And beautiful beyond compare . . .
But you reached out your arms for more
To catch what you were yearning for,
But little did you think or guess
That one can't capture happiness
Because it's unrestrained and free,
Unfettered by reality.

The Golden Chain of Friendship

Friendship is a golden chain,
   the links are friends so dear,
And like a rare and precious jewel,
   it's treasured more each year.
It's clasped together firmly
   with a love that's deep and true,
And it's rich with happy memories
   and fond recollections, too.
Time can't destroy its beauty,
   for as long as memory lives,
Years can't erase the pleasure
   that the joy of friendship gives . . .
For friendship is a priceless gift
   that can't be bought or sold,
And to have an understanding friend
   is worth far more than gold . . .
And the golden chain of friendship
   is a strong and blessed tie
Binding kindred hearts together
   as the years go passing by.

The Gift of Friendship

Friendship is a priceless gift
    that cannot be bought or sold,
But its value is far greater
    than a mountain made of gold—
For gold is cold and lifeless,
    it can neither see nor hear,
And in the time of trouble
    it is powerless to cheer.
It has no ears to listen,
    no heart to understand,
It cannot bring you comfort
    or reach out a helping hand—
So when you ask God for a gift
    be thankful if He sends
Not diamonds, pearls, or riches,
    but the love of real true friends.

Friends Are Life's Gift of Love

If people like me
    didn't know people like you,
Life would lose its meaning
    and its richness, too . . .
For the friends that we make
    are life's gift of love,
And I think friends are sent
    right from heaven above . . .
And thinking of you
    somehow makes me feel
That God is love
    and He's very real.

Just Friends

Like ships upon the sea of life
We meet with friends so dear,
Then sail on swiftly from the ones
We'd like to linger near;
Sometimes I wish
The winds would cease,
The waves be quiet too,
And let me sort of drift along
Beside a friend like you.

Verse from very early greeting cards in the Helen Steiner Rice Foundation archives.

Life Is a Garden

Life is a garden,
    good friends are the flowers,
And times spent together
    life's happiest hours . . .
And friendship, like flowers,
    blooms ever more fair
When carefully tended
    by dear friends who care . . .
And life's lovely garden
    would be sweeter by far
If all who passed through it
    were as nice as you are.

The Garden of Friendship

There is no garden
So complete
But roses could make
The place more sweet.
There is no life
So rich and rare
But one more friend
Could enter there.
Like roses in a garden
Kindness fills the air
With a certain bit of sweetness
As it touches everywhere.

Love

What Is Love?

What is love? No words can define it—
It's something so great only God could design it.
Wonder of wonders, beyond man's conception—
And only in God can love find true perfection . . .
For love means much more than small words can express,
For what man calls love is so very much less
Than the beauty and depth and the true richness of
God's gift to mankind of compassion from above
For love has become a word that's misused,
Perverted, distorted, and often abused
To speak of light romance or some affinity for,
A passing attraction that is seldom much more
Than a mere interlude of inflamed fascination,
A romantic fling of no lasting duration . . .
But love is enduring and patient and kind—
It judges all with the heart, not the mind . . .
And love can transform the most commonplace
Into beauty and splendor and sweetness and grace . . .
For love is unselfish, giving more than it takes—
And no matter what happens love never forsakes.
It's faithful and trusting and always believing,
Guileless and honest and never deceiving.
Yes, love is beyond what man can define,
For love is immortal and God's gift is divine!

Deep in My Heart

Happy little memories
   go flitting through my mind,
And in all my thoughts and memories
   I always seem to find
The picture of your face, dear,
   the memory of your touch,
And all the other little things
   I've come to love so much.
You cannot go beyond my thoughts
   or leave my love behind
Because I keep you in my heart
   and forever on my mind . . .
And though I may not tell you,
   I think you know it's true
That I find daily happiness
   in the very thought of you.

The Gift of a Lasting Love

Love is much more than a tender caress
And more than bright hours of happiness,
For a lasting love is made up of sharing
Both hours that are joyous and also despairing.
It's made up of patience and deep understanding
And never of stubborn or selfish demanding.
It's made up of climbing the steep hills together
And facing with courage life's stormiest weather.
And nothing on earth or in heaven can part
A love that has grown to be part of the heart
And just like the sun and the stars and the sea,
This love will go on through eternity,
For true love lives on when earthly things die,
For it's part of the spirit that soars to the sky.

Romance

I'd like to be a rain-drop
Just falling on your hand,
I'd like to be a blade of grass
On which your dear feet stand,
I'd like to be your shadow
As it moves around all day,
I'd like to be most anything
That hangs around your way.

Sweetheart

You're lovable, you're wonderful,
You're as sweet as you can be,
There's nobody in all the world
Could mean so much to me;
I love you more than life itself,
You make my dreams come true,
Forever is not long enough
For me to be near to you.

Heartstrings

Pleasant little memories
   tuggin' at my heart
Keep me thinkin' of you
   when we are apart,
And, with every heart-tug,
   wishes sweet and true
Leave my heart's door open,
   and find their way to you,
But I don't mind the tuggin'
   at my heartstrings all year through
Because it's mighty pleasant
   when it's being done by you.

These three poems are from very early greeting cards in the Helen
Steiner Rice Foundation archives.

Where There Is Love

Where there is love the heart is light,
Where there is love the day is bright.
Where there is love there is a song
To help when things are going wrong.
Where there is love there is a smile
To make all things seem more worthwhile.
Where there is love there's a quiet peace—
A tranquil place where turmoils cease.
Love changes darkness into light
And makes the heart take wingless flight.
Oh, blessed are those who walk in love—
They also walk with God above . . .
And when you walk with God each day
And kneel together when you pray,
Your marriage will be truly blessed
And God will be your daily guest,
And love that once seemed yours alone
God gently blends into His own.

Wings of Love

The priceless gift of life is love,
For with the help of God above
Love can change the human race
And make this world a better place . . .
For love dissolves all hate and fear
And makes our vision bright and clear
So we can see and rise above
Our pettiness on wings of love.

The Magic of Love

Love is like magic
    and it always will be,
For love still remains
    life's sweet mystery.
Love works in ways
    that are wondrous and strange,
And there's nothing in life
    that love cannot change.
Love can transform
    the most commonplace
Into beauty and splendor
    and sweetness and grace.
Love is unselfish,
    understanding, and kind,
For it sees with its heart
    and not with its mind.
Love gives and forgives—
    there is nothing too much
For love to heal
    with its magic touch.
Love is the language
    that every heart speaks,
For love is the one thing
    that every heart seeks . . .
And where there is love
    God too will abide
And bless the family
    residing inside.

God's Love Is a Haven in the Storms of Life

God's love is like an island
    in life's ocean vast and wide—
A peaceful, quiet shelter
    from the restless, rising tide.
God's love is like a fortress,
    and we seek protection there
When the waves of tribulation
    seem to drown us in despair.
God's love's a sanctuary
    where our souls can find sweet rest
From the struggle and the tension
    of life's fast and futile quest.
God's love is like a tower
    rising far above the crowd,
And God's smile is like the sunshine
    breaking through a threatening cloud.
God's love is like a beacon
    burning bright with faith and prayer,
And through the changing scenes of life
    we can find a haven there.
For God's love is fashioned
    after something enduring
And it is endless and unfailing
    like His character above.

Celebrations

A New Year's Eve Prayer

What better time and what better season,
What greater occasion or more wonderful reason
To kneel down in prayer and lift our hands high
To the God of creation, who made earth and sky,
Who sent us His Son to live here among men—
And the message He brought is as true now as then . . .
So at this glad season, when there's joy everywhere,
Let us meet our Redeemer at the altar of prayer,
Asking Him humbly to bless all of our days
And grant us forgiveness for our erring ways . . .
And though we're unworthy, dear Father above,
Accept us today and let us dwell in Thy love
So we may grow stronger upheld by Thy grace,
And with Thy assistance be ready to face
All the temptations that fill every day,
And hold on to our hands when we stumble and stray . . .
And thank You, dear God, for the year that now ends
And for the great blessing of loved ones and friends.

A New Year Brings a New Beginning

As the new year starts and the old year ends,
There's no better time for making amends
For all the things we sincerely regret
And wish in our hearts we could somehow forget.
We all make mistakes—it's human to err—
But no one need ever give up in despair,
For God gives us all a brand-new beginning,
A chance to start over and repent of our sinning . . .
And when God forgives us, we too must forgive
And resolve to do better each day that we live
By constantly trying to be like Him more nearly
And to trust in His wisdom and to love Him more dearly—
Assured that we're never out of His care
And we're always welcome to seek Him in prayer.

Birthdays Are Gateways

Birthdays come and birthdays go
And with them comes the thought
Of all the happy memories
That passing years have brought,
And looking back across the years
We come to recognize
That it takes a lot of birthdays
To make us kind and wise,
For growing older only means
The spirit grows serene
And we behold things with our souls
That our eyes have never seen.
For each birthday is a gateway
That leads to a reward,
The rich reward of learning,
The true greatness of the Lord.

God's Unfailing Birthday Promise

From one birthday to another
    God will gladly give
To everyone who seeks Him
    and tries each day to live
A little bit more closely
    to God and to each other,
Seeing everyone who passes
    as a neighbor, friend, or brother,
Not only joy and happiness
    but the faith to meet each trial
Not with fear and trepidation
    but with an inner smile . . .
For we know life's never measured
    by how many years we live
But by the kindly things we do
    and the happiness we give.

When You Are Young, Birthdays Are Wonderful

You are young, and life is beginning
    in a wonderful way for you.
The future reaches its welcoming hand
    with new, challenging things to do . . .
And here is a prayer for your birthday
    that you'll walk with God every day,
Remembering always in whatever you do
    there is only one true, righteous way . . .
For God, in His wisdom and mercy,
    looked down on His children below
And gave them the privilege of choosing
    the right or the wrong way to go . . .
So trust in His almighty wisdom
    and enjoy the fruit of His love,
And life on earth will be happy
    as you walk with the Father above.

Just for You on Your Birthday

There are some that we meet in passing
    and forget them as soon as they go—
There are some we remember with pleasure
    and feel honored and privileged to know . . .
And you are that kind of person
    who leaves lovely memories behind,
And special days like your birthday
    bring many fond memories to mind . . .
And memories are priceless possessions
    that time can never destroy,
For it is in happy remembrance
    that the heart finds its greatest joy.

Birthday Blues

When your axle is a draggin'
And your tires are wearin' thin,
Then birthdays aren't something
That you welcome with a grin.
And I'm speaking from experience
Although it's sad but true,
Father Time and Mother Nature
Sure can make it tough for you.
I'll admit I'm getting mildewed
And my carburetor's busted,
My chassis's cracked and dented
And my spark plugs all are rusted.
But what's the use of griping
Because we've stripped our gears?
You can't expect to feel like twenty
When you've lived over fifty years.
Happy Birthday, dear friend.

From very early greeting card verse in the Helen Steiner Rice Foundation archives.

Birthdays Are a Gift from God

Where does time go in its endless flight?
Spring turns to fall and day to night,
And birthdays come and birthdays go,
And where they go we do not know . . .
But God, who planned our life on earth
And gave our minds and bodies birth
And then enclosed a living soul
With heaven as the spirit's goal,
Has given man the gift of choice
To follow that small inner voice
That speaks to us from year to year,
Reminding us we've naught to fear . . .

For birthdays are a stepping stone
To endless joys as yet unknown—
So fill each day with happy things,
And may your burdens all take wing
And fly away and leave behind
Great joy of heart and peace of mind . . .
For birthdays are the gateway to
An endless life of joy for you
If you but pray from day to day
That He will show you the truth and the way.

A Graduate's Prayer

Father, I have knowledge,
    so will You show me now
How to use it wisely
    and to find a way somehow
To make the world I live in
    a little better place
And to make life with its problems
    a bit easier to face?
Grant me faith and courage,
    and put purpose in my days,
And show me how to serve Thee
    in the most effective ways,
So all my education,
    my knowledge and my skill
May find their true fulfillment
    if I learn to do Thy will . . .
And may I ever be aware
    in everything I do
That knowledge comes from learning,
    and wisdom comes from You.

My Father's Day Prayer

I said a Father's Day prayer for you—
 I asked the Lord above
To keep you safely in His care
 and enfold you in His love . . .
I did not ask for fortune,
 for riches or for fame,
I only asked for blessings
 in the Holy Savior's name—
Blessings to surround you
 in times of trial and stress,
And inner joy to fill your heart
 with peace and happiness.

A Mother's Day Prayer

Our Father in heaven,
 whose love is divine,
Thanks for the love
 of a mother like mine.
In Thy great mercy
 look down from above
And grant this dear mother
 the gift of Your love,
And all through the year,
 whatever betide her,
Assure her each day
 that You are beside her . . .
And, Father in heaven,
 show me the way
To lighten her tasks
 and brighten her day,
And bless her dear heart
 with the insight to see
That her love means more
 than the world to me.

For a Young Person at Confirmation

When we are confirmed
   in our faith in the Lord,
Our greatest possession
   and richest reward
Is knowing that now
   we are heralds of the King,
Ready His praises
   and glory to sing . . .
And oh, what a privilege
   to witness for God
And to walk in the way
   that the dear Savior trod—
Confirmed in the faith
   and upheld by His hand,
Eager to follow
   His smallest command,
Secure in the knowledge
   that though now and then
We're guilty of sins
   that are common to men,
He freely forgives
   and understands, too,
And there's nothing—
   no nothing that God cannot do . . .
And great is our gladness
   to serve Him through others,
For our Father taught us
   that all men are brothers,
And the people we meet
   on life's thoroughfares
Are burdened with trouble
   and sorrow and cares,

And this is the chance
  we are given each day
To witness for God
  and to try to obey
His laws and commandments,
  and to make our Confirmation
A service of joy
  and a real dedication.

A Prayer for the Bride and Groom

As hand in hand you enter
  a life that's bright and new,
May God look down from heaven
  and bless the two of you.
May He give you understanding,
  enough to make you kind,
So you may judge each other
  with your hearts and not your minds.
May He teach you to be patient
  as you learn to live together,
Forgiving little human rifts
  that arise in stormy weather . . .
And may your love be strong enough
  to withstand the strongest sea,
So you may dwell forever
  in love's rich tranquility.

A Prayer for the Bride

Oh, God of love look down and bless
This radiant bride with happiness,
And fill her life with love's sweet song,
Enough to last her whole life long . . .
And give her patience when things disturb
So she can somehow gently curb
Hasty words in anger spoken,
Leaving two hearts sad and broken . . .
And give her guidance all through life
And keep her a loving, faithful wife.

May God Bless Your Wedding Day

May God bless your wedding day
   and every day thereafter
And fill your home with happiness
   and your hearts with love and laughter . . .
And may each year together
   find you more and more in love
And bring you all the happiness
   you're so deserving of.
May the joy of true companionship
   be yours to share through life,
And may you always bless the day
   that made you husband and wife.

A Prayer for the Newlyweds

As you enter into the little world
that you have promised
to make brighter for each other
may He who harnesses the waves
and hangs the sun out in the sky

and puts the song in birds
especially bless you
and make your marriage
a good and happy one.

Another Link of Love

It takes a special day like this
To just look back and reminisce
And think of things you've shared together
Through sunny, fair, and stormy weather,
And how both smiles as well as tears
Endear true love across the years . . .
For there is no explaining of
The mystery of the bond of love,
Which just grows richer, deeper, stronger
Because you've shared it one year longer.

Happy Anniversary

It's been many years
    since you both said "I do,"
And surely lots has happened
    to both of you,
For you can't live together
    for all of those years
And never dampen your smiles
    with at least a few tears . . .
And only through years
    of patience and sharing
Do you earn the priceless
    and rich joy of caring.
And these happy years
    so devotedly spent
Now bring you a harvest
    of peace and content.

Silver Anniversary

Another anniversary
    marks another year of life,
Another year of sharing
    as husband and as wife . . .
And sending you good wishes
    is a happy thing to do,
For there is no greater pleasure
    than knowing folks like you
Who through love and understanding
    have gone along life's way,
So it's a joy to celebrate
    your silver wedding day.

God among Us—
Christmas and
Easter

This Is the Savior of the World

All the world has heard the story
    of the little Christ Child's birth,
But too few have felt the meaning
    of His mission here on earth.
Some regard the Christmas story
    as something beautiful to hear,
A lovely Christmas custom
    that we celebrate each year,
But it is more than just a story
    told to make our hearts rejoice—
It's our Father up in heaven
    speaking through the Christ Child's voice,
Telling us of heavenly kingdoms
    that He has prepared above
For all who trust His mercy
    and live only for His love . . .
And only through the Christ Child
    can man be born again,
For God sent the Baby Jesus
    as the Savior of all men.

The Gift of God's Love

All over the world at this season,
    expectant hands reach to receive
Gifts that are lavishly fashioned—
    the finest that man can conceive . . .
For purchased and given at Christmas
    are luxuries we long to possess,
Given as favors and tokens
    to try in some way to express
That strange, indefinable feeling
    which is part of this glad time of year

When streets are crowded with shoppers
   and the air resounds with good cheer . . .
But back of each tinsel-tied package
   exchanged at this gift-giving season,
Unrecognized often by many,
   lies a deeper, more meaningful reason—
For, born in a manger at Christmas
   as a gift from the Father above,
An Infant whose name was called Jesus
   brought mankind the gift of God's love . . .
And the gifts that we give have no purpose
   unless God is part of the giving
And unless we make Christmas a pattern
   to be followed in everyday living.

Christmastime Is Friendship Time

At Christmastime our hearts reach out
   to friends we think of dearly,
And checking through our friendship lists,
   as all of us do yearly,
We stop a while to reminisce
   and to pleasantly review
Happy little happenings
   and things we used to do . . .
And though we've been too busy
   to keep in touch all year,
We send a Christmas greeting
   at this season of good cheer . . .
So Christmas is a lovely link
   between old years and new
That keeps the bond of friendship
   forever unbroken and true.

The Comfort of His Love

A baby was born in a manger
While a bright star shone down from above
And the world learned the depths of God's mercy
And the comfort and strength of His love.
May the thought of that long ago Christmas
And the meaning it's sure to impart,
Bring a wonderful message of comfort
And a deep new peace to your heart.

If Thou Knewest the Gift of God

Christmas is a gift of love
    that can't be bought or sold—
It's ours just for the asking,
    and it's worth far more than gold.
And this priceless gift of Christmas
    is within the reach of all—
The rich, the poor, the young, the old,
    the greatest and the small.
So take God's Christmas gift of love—
    reach out and you receive—
And the only payment that God asks
    is just that you believe.
Christmas is a heavenly gift
    that only God can give—
It's ours just for the asking
    for as long as we shall live.
It can't be bought or bartered,
    it can't be won or sold,
It doesn't cost a penny,
    and it's worth far more than gold.
It isn't bright and gleaming
    for eager eyes to see—

It can't be wrapped in tinsel
or placed beneath a tree . . .
For the priceless gift of Christmas
is meant just for the heart,
And we receive it only
when we become a part
Of the kingdom and the glory
which is ours to freely take,
For God sent the holy Christ Child
at Christmas for our sake.
So take His priceless gift of love—
reach out and you receive—
And the only payment that God asks
is just that you believe.

This poem combines favorite lines from several other Helen Steiner
Rice poems, a practice Mrs. Rice sometimes used when pressured to
produce new verse on demand.

The Spirit of Giving

Each year at Christmas, the spirit of giving
Adds joy to the season and gladness to living.
Knowing this happens when Christmas is here,
Why can't we continue throughout the year
To make our lives happy and abundant with living
By following each day the spirit of giving?

The Priceless Gift of Christmas, version 1

Now Christmas is a season for joy and merrymaking,
A time for gifts and presents, for giving and for taking,
A festive, friendly, happy time when everyone is gay—
But have we ever really felt the greatness of the day?
For through the centuries the world has wandered far away
From the beauty and the meaning of the holy Christmas Day
For Christmas is a heavenly gift that only God can give—
It's ours just for the asking for as long as we shall live.
It can't be bought or bartered, it can't be won or sold,
It doesn't cost a penny, and it's worth far more than gold.
It isn't bright and gleaming for eager eyes to see—
It can't be wrapped in tinsel or placed beneath a tree.
It isn't soft and shimmering for reaching hands to touch,
Or some expensive luxury you've wanted very much.
For the priceless gift of Christmas is meant just for the heart,
And we receive it only when we become a part
Of the kingdom and the glory which is ours to freely take,
For God sent the holy Christ Child at Christmas for our sake
So man might come to know Him and feel His presence near
And see the many miracles performed when He was here.
And this priceless gift of Christmas is within the reach of all—
The rich, the poor, the young and old, the greatest and the small.
So take His priceless gift of love—reach out and you receive—
And the only payment that God asks is just that you believe.

One of Helen Steiner Rice's most popular poems, "The Priceless Gift of Christmas," was worked and reworked in several variations. These two remain the most popular.

The Priceless Gift of Christmas, version 2

Christmas is a heavenly gift that only God can give—
It's ours just for the asking for as long as we shall live.
The priceless gift of Christmas is meant just for the heart,
And we receive it only when we become a part

Of the kingdom and the glory which is ours to freely take,
For God sent the holy Christ Child at Christmas for our sake . . .
So man might come to know Him and feel His presence near
And see the many miracles performed when He was here.
This priceless gift of Christmas is within the reach of all—
The rich, the poor, the young and old, the greatest and the small.
So take His priceless gift of love—reach out and you receive,
And the only payment that God asks is just that you believe.

Christmas Is a Season for Giving

Christmas is a season
   for gifts of every kind—
All the glittery, pretty things
   that Christmas shoppers find—
Baubles, beads, and bangles
   of silver and of gold—
Anything and everything
   that can be bought or sold
Is given at this season
   to place beneath the tree,
For Christmas is a special time
   for giving lavishly.
But there's one rare and priceless gift
   that can't be sold or bought—
It's something poor or rich can give,
   for it's a loving thought . . .
And loving thoughts are blessings
   for which no one can pay,
And only loving hearts can give
   this priceless gift away.

This Is What Christmas Means to Me

Christmas to me is a gift from above—
A gift of salvation born of God's love—
For far beyond what my mind comprehends,
My eternal future completely depends
On that first Christmas night centuries ago
When God sent His Son to the earth below—
For if the Christ Child had not been born,
There would be no rejoicing on Easter morn.
For only because Christ was born and died
And hung on a cross to be crucified
Can worldly sinners like you and me
Be fit to live in eternity.
So Christmas is more than getting and giving—
It's the why and wherefore of infinite living.
It's the positive proof for doubting God never,
For in His kingdom, life is forever . . .
And this is the reason that on Christmas Day
I can only kneel and prayerfully say,
"Thank You, God, for sending Your Son
So that when my work on earth is done
I can look at last on Your holy face,
Knowing You saved me alone by Your grace."

Behold

Glad tidings herald the Christ Child's birth—
"Joy to the World" and "Peace on Earth,"
"Glory to God" . . . Let all men rejoice
And hearken once more to the angel's voice.
It matters not who or what you are—
All men can behold the Christmas star,
For the star that shone is shining still
In the hearts of men of peace and good will.

It offers the answer to every man's need,
Regardless of color or race or creed . . .
So, joining together in brotherly love,
Let us worship again our Father above,
And, forgetting our own little, selfish desires,
May we seek what the star of Christmas inspires.

Glory to God

"Glory to God in the highest,
    and on earth peace, good will toward men."
May the angels' song of long ago
    ring in our hearts again
And bring a new awareness
    that the fate of every nation
Is sealed securely in the hand
    of the Maker of creation . . .
For man, with all his knowledge,
    his wisdom, and his skill,
Is powerless to go beyond
    the holy Father's will . . .
And when we fully recognize
    the helplessness of man
And seek our Father's guidance
    in our every thought and plan,
Then only can we build a world
    of faith and hope and love,
And only then can man achieve
    the life he's dreaming of.

A Prayer for Christmas

God, give us eyes this Christmas
    to see the Christmas star,
And give us ears to hear the song
    of angels from afar . . .
And with our eyes and ears attuned
    for a message from above,
Let Christmas angels speak to us
    of hope and faith and love—
Hope to light our pathway
    when the way ahead is dark,
Hope to sing through stormy days
    with the sweetness of a lark,
Faith to trust in things unseen
    and know beyond all seeing
That it is in our Father's love
    we live and have our being,
And love to break down barriers
    of color, race, and creed,
Love to see and understand
    and help all those in need.

Every Year When Christmas Comes

I have a list of folks I know all written in a book
And every year when Christmas comes, I go and take a look.
And that is when I realize that these names are a part
Not of the book they're written in, but of my very heart.
And while it sounds fantastic for me to make this claim
I really feel that I'm composed of each remembered name,
So never think my Christmas cards are just a mere routine
Of names upon a Christmas list forgotten in between,

For I am but the total of the many folks I've met
And you happen to be one of those I prefer to not forget.
And every year when Christmas comes, I realize anew
The best gift life can offer is meeting folks like you—
And may the spirit of Christmas that forevermore endures
Leave its richest blessings in the hearts of you and yours.

A Christmas Wish

At Christmas and always,
may you be guided by His light
and surrounded with His love.

More Christmas Wishes

At Christmas may God grant you
Special gifts of joy and cheer,
And bless you for the good you do
For others through the year . . .
May you find rich satisfaction
In your daily work and prayer,
And in knowing as you serve Him
He will keep you in His care.

Wishes for This Christmas

May this Christmas season bring you
Many blessings from above,
And may the coming year be filled
With peace and joy and love.

Christmas Thanks

This comes to you with loving thoughts
When Christmastime is here—
Thoughts of all the qualities
That make you very dear . . .
And this brings you many wishes
That today and always, too,
You'll have the special happiness
That ought to come to you.

May Christmas Come Again and Again

Here's hoping that your Christmas
Is a time that's set apart—
A time that's filled with happiness
And sunshine in your heart . . .
And may the warmth and love you give
Return to you all year
To brighten days in many ways
And fill your life with cheer!

Why Write These Christmas Greetings?

I wonder if you know the real reason
I send you a card every year at this season?
Do you think it's a habit I just can't break
Or something I do just for custom's sake?
I think I should tell you it's something more
For to me Christmas opens the friendship door . . .
And I find myself reaching across the year
And clasping the hand of somebody dear.
To me it's a link I wouldn't want broken
That holds us together when words are unspoken.
For oft through the year we have to forego

Exchanging good wishes with those we know,
But Christmas opens the door of the heart
And whether we're close or far apart . . .
When I write your name I think of you
And pause and reflect and always renew
The bond that exists since we first met
And I found you somebody too nice to forget.

Christmas and the Christ Child

In our Christmas celebrations
    of merriment and mirth,
Let us not forget the miracle
    of the holy Christ Child's birth . . .
For in our festivities
    it is easy to lose sight
Of the Baby in the manger
    and that holy, silent night . . .
And we miss the mighty meaning
    and we lose the greater glory
Of the holy little Christ Child
    and the blessed Christmas story
If we don't keep Christ in Christmas
    and make His love a part
Of all the joy and happiness
    that fill our homes and hearts.

What Is Christmas?

Is it just a day at the end of the year—
A season of joy, merrymaking, and cheer?
Is it people and presents and glittering trees?
Oh no, it is more than any of these,
For under the tinsel and hidden from sight
Is the promise and meaning of that first Christmas night
When the shepherds stood in wondered awe
And felt transformed by what they saw.
So let us not in our search for pleasure
Forego our right to this priceless treasure,
For Christmas is still a God-given day,
And let us remember to keep it that way.

A Beautiful Beginning for Peace on Earth

Let us all remember
　　when our faith is running low,
Christ is more than just a figure
　　wrapped in an ethereal glow . . .
For He came and dwelled among us
　　and He knows our every need,
And He loves and understands us
　　and forgives each sinful deed.
He was crucified and buried
　　and rose again in glory,
And His promise of salvation
　　makes the wondrous Christmas story
An abiding reassurance
　　that the little Christ Child's birth
Was the beautiful beginning
　　of God's plan for peace on earth.

May Christmas Renew in Us a Childlike Faith

May Christmas renew in us a childlike faith
For only then can we all endure
These changing times and feel secure,
For faith in things we cannot see
Requires a child's simplicity—
For in a small child's shining eyes
The faith of all the ages lies . . .
And tiny hands and tousled heads
That kneel in prayer by little beds
Are closer to the dear Lord's heart
And of His kingdom more a part
Than we who search and never find
The answers to our questioning minds—
For God can never be defined
By any meager, mortal mind,
And only a child can completely accept
What probing adults research and reject.
O Father, grant once more to men
A simple, childlike faith again,
For only by faith and faith alone
Can we approach our Father's throne.

A Christmas Blessing

May Jesus, our Savior,
    Who was born on Christmas Day,
Bless you at this season
    in a very special way.
May the beauty and the promise
    of that silent, holy night
Fill your heart with peace and happiness
    and make your new year bright.

Discovering Christmas

May Christmas this year, amid chaos, cruelty and conflict,
be a blessed instrument through which we can find
comfort, courage, and cheer in the communion of our
   hearts.
May we discover this Christmas,
the sustaining powers of a strong faith
and the abiding values of courage,
heroism, honor, fellowship, and freedom.
May our material gifts be less
and our spiritual gifts greater.
"Peace on earth, good will to all"
is not an empty dream.
It is the miracle of Christmas and
such miracles are made of faith and brave hearts.
May God bless you
and may the New Year find us all
not only safe, but free.

From a personal Christmas message by Mrs. Rice on December 25,
1942.

May the Star Shine in Your Heart

May the holy remembrance
   of that first Christmas night
Make this blessed season
   more joyous and bright . . .
And may the Star of Bethlehem,
   which shone down from above,
Keep shining in your heart today
   and in the hearts of those you love.

A Christmas Prayer

O God, our help in ages past,
  our hope in years to be,
Look down upon this present
  and see our need of Thee . . .
For in this age of unrest,
  with danger all around,
We need Thy hand to lead us
  to a higher, safer ground.
We need Thy help and counsel
  to make us more aware
That our safety and security
  lie solely in Thy care,
And so we pray this Christmas
  to feel Thy presence near
And for Thy all-wise guidance
  throughout the coming year.
First, give us understanding,
  enough to make us kind,
So we may judge all people
  with our hearts and not our minds.
Then give us strength and courage
  to be honorable and true,
And place our trust implicitly
  in unseen things and You . . .
And help us when we falter
  and renew our faith each day
And forgive our human errors
  and hear us when we pray,
And keep us gently humble
  in the greatness of Thy love
So someday we are fit to dwell
  with Thee in peace above.

A Prayer for Christmas Every Day

Oh, Father up in heaven,
    we have wandered far away
From the little holy Christ Child
    that was born on Christmas Day,
And the peace on earth you promised
    we have been unmindful of,
Not believing we could find it
    in a simple thing called love.
We've forgotten why You sent us
    Jesus Christ, Your only Son,
And in arrogance and ignorance
    it's our will, not Thine, be done.
Oh, forgive us, heavenly Father,
    teach us how to be more kind
So that we may judge all people
    with our hearts and not our minds . . .
Oh, forgive us, heavenly Father,
    and help us to find the way
To understand each other
    and live Christmas every day.

God Is Everywhere

Our Father up in heaven,
    long, long years ago,
Looked down in His great mercy
    upon the earth below
And saw that folks were lonely
    and lost in deep despair,
And so He said, "I'll send My Son
    to walk among them there
So they can hear Him speaking
    and feel His nearness, too,
And see the many miracles
    that faith alone can do . . .

For if man really sees Him
   and can touch His healing hand,
I know it will be easier
   to believe and understand."
And so the holy Christ Child
   came down to live on earth,
And that is why we celebrate
   His holy, wondrous birth . . .
And that is why at Christmas
   the world becomes aware
That heaven may seem far away,
   but God is everywhere.

The Christmas Story

Some regard the Christmas story
   as something beautiful to hear—
A dramatized tradition
   that's retold from year to year,
But it is more than just a story—
   it's God's promise to all men
That only through the Christ Child
   can man be born again.
It's God's assurance of a future
   beyond all that man has dreamed,
For Jesus lived on earth and died
   so that man might be redeemed—
And eternal is the kingdom
   that God has prepared above
For all who trust His mercy
   and dwell daily in His love.
Mankind's hope and his salvation
   are in the Christmas story,
For in these words there are revealed
   God's greatness and His glory.

Gloria in Excelsis Deo

A star in the sky, an angel's voice
Telling the world—Rejoice! Rejoice!
Shepherds tending their flocks by night,
Falling in awe at this wondrous sight,
Wise men traveling across the lands
To place their gifts in the Christ Child's hands,
No room at the inn, so a manger bed
Cradled in radiance the holy Babe's head . . .
That is the story that's living still
In the hearts of all men who seek peace and good will.
But in selfishness and vanity we have wandered far away
From the holy little Christ Child who was born on Christmas Day,
But to find the peace God promised, we must return again
To the Baby in the manger, who was born to save all men.
And life on earth has not been the same, regardless of what the
    skeptics claim,
For no event ever left behind a transformation of this kind . . .
So question and search and doubt if you will, but the story of
    Christmas is living still.

May God Dwell in Us Again

There is no thinking person who can stand untouched today
And view the world around us slowly drifting to decay
Without feeling deep within him a silent, unnamed dread
As he contemplates the future that lies frighteningly ahead . . .
For like watching storm clouds gather in a dark and threatening sky,
Man knows that there is nothing he can formulate or try
That will stop the storm from breaking in its fury and its force,
Nor can he change or alter the storm's destructive course,
But his anxious fears are lessened when he calls on God above,
For he knows above the storm cloud is the brightness of God's love . . .

So as the clouds of chaos gather in man's muddled mind
And he searches for the answer he alone can never find,
Let us recognize we're facing problems man has never solved,
And with all our daily efforts life grows more and more involved . . .
But our future will seem brighter and we'll meet with less resistance
If we call upon our Father and seek divine assistance,
For the spirit can unravel many tangled, knotted threads
That defy the skill and power of the world's best hands and heads,
And our plans for growth and progress, of which we all have dreamed,
Cannot survive materially unless our spirits are redeemed . . .
So may our prayer this Christmas be that God may dwell again
In human hearts throughout the world and bring good will to men.

A Christmas Prayer for Peace

We pray to Thee, our Father,
   as Christmas comes again,
For peace among all nations
   and good will between all men.
Give us the strength and courage
   to search ourselves inside
And recognize our vanity,
   our selfishness and pride . . .
For the struggle of all ages
   is centered deep within,
Where each man has his private war
   that his own soul must win . . .
For a world of peace and plenty,
   of which all men have dreamed,
Can only be attained and kept
   when the spirit is redeemed.

Only with Our Hearts

With our eyes we see
the glitter of Christmas,
  with our ears we hear
  its merriment,
    with our hands we touch
    the tinsel-tied trinkets . . .
  but only with our hearts can we feel
    the miracle of it.

The Miracle of Christmas

The wonderment in a small child's eyes,
The ageless awe in the Christmas skies,
The nameless joy that fills the air,
The throngs that kneel in praise and prayer—
These are the things that make us know
That men may come and men may go,
But none will ever find a way
To banish Christ from Christmas Day,
For with each child there's born again
A mystery that baffles men.

Thoughts for Your Easter

The miracles of Easter
Bespeak divine perfection,
And they are a living evidence
Of our Savior's resurrection.
Like beads upon a rosary,
Each thought becomes a prayer—
May God bless you at Easter
And keep you in His care.
Hope your Easter's happy,
Hope your springtime's bright,
Hope your skies are sunny,

And hope your heart is light!
Easter is a season
Of fulfillment for the soul,
A time of reaching upward
Toward a heavenly goal.
Easter and spring
Are God's loving way
Of showing that He
Is still with us today.

The Hope of the World

An empty tomb, a stone rolled away
Speak of the Savior who rose Easter Day,
But that was centuries and centuries ago
And we ask today—Was it really so?
Did He walk on earth and live and die
And return to His Father to dwell on high?
We were not there to hear or see,
But our hopes and dreams of eternity
Are centered around the Easter story
When Christ ascended and rose in glory,
And life on earth has not been the same
Regardless of what the skeptics claim.
For after the Lord was crucified,
Even the ones who had scoffed and denied
Knew that something had taken place
That nothing could ever remove or erase . . .
For hope was born in the soul of man,
And faith to believe in God's master plan
Stirred in the hearts to dispel doubt and fear,
And that faith has grown with each passing year.
For the hope of man is the Easter story,
And life is robbed of all meaning and glory
Unless man knows that he has a goal
And a resting place for his searching soul.

In the Garden of Gethsemane

Before the dawn of Easter
There came Gethsemane . . .
Before the Resurrection
There were hours of agony . . .
For there can be no crown of stars
Without a cross to bear,
And there is no salvation
Without faith and love and prayer,
And when we take our needs to God
Let us pray as did His Son
That dark night in Gethsemane—
"Thy will, not mine, be done."

The Blessed Assurance of Easter

Easter means beauty
    and new life and spring.
It means the awakening
    of each sleeping thing,
And in that awakening
    the world sees again
The promise of life
    God gave to all men . . .
For God sent His Son
    to bless and to save
And redeem us from sin
    and death and the grave.

Rejoice! It's Easter!

Easter is a season of fulfillment
    that the heart is longing for,
And the promise of salvation
    was never needed more.

An Easter View

Easter is a season
  of hope and joy and cheer—
There's beauty all around us
  to see and touch and hear . . .
So no matter how downhearted
  and discouraged we may be,
New hope is born when we behold
  leaves budding on a tree,
And troubles seem to vanish
  when robins start to sing,
For God never sends the winter
  without the joy of spring.

Reaching Upward

Easter is a season
  of fulfillment for the soul,
A time of reaching upward
  toward a heavenly goal,
A time for recognizing
  that our lives are in God's hand,
And, trusting in His mercy,
  we need not understand.

He Lives

He lives in the beauty
  that comes with spring—
The Easter lilies,
  the birds that sing—
And He lives in people
  as nice as you,
And He lives in all
  the nice things you do.

An Easter Wish

Here's hoping that your Easter
Is delightful from the start—
A day that's filled with happiness
And sunshine in your heart.
And may the special warmth you show
Return to you all year
To brighten days in many ways
And fill your life with cheer!

Peace

If we could just lift up our hearts
Like flowers to the sun
And trust His Easter promise
And pray, "Thy will be done,"
We'd find the peace we're seeking,
The kind no man can give—
The peace that comes from knowing
He died so we might live!

Partakers of His Glory

"Let not your heart be troubled"—
Let not your soul be sad.
Easter is a time of joy
When all hearts should be glad—
Glad to know that Jesus Christ
Made it possible for men
To have their sins forgiven
And, like Him, to live again . . .
So at this joyous season
May the wondrous Easter story
Renew our faith so we may be
Partakers of His glory.

An Easter Meditation

In the glorious Easter story,
    a troubled world can find
Blessed reassurance
    and enduring peace of mind . . .
For though we grow discouraged
    with this world we're living in,
There is comfort just in knowing
    God has triumphed over sin . . .
For our Savior's resurrection
    was God's way of telling men
That in Christ we are eternal
    and in Him we live again . . .
And to know life is unending
    and God's love is endless, too,
Makes our daily tasks and burdens
    so much easier to do . . .
And our earthly trials and troubles
    are but guideposts on the way
To the love and life eternal
    that God promised Easter Day.

In Christ All Men May Live Again

Let us all remember
　　when our faith is running low,
Christ is more than just a figure
　　wrapped in an ethereal glow.
For He came and dwelled among us
　　and He knows our every need,
And He loves and understands us
　　and forgives each sinful deed.
He was crucified and buried
　　and rose again in glory,
And the Savior's resurrection
　　makes the wondrous Easter story
An abiding reassurance
　　that man dies to live again
In a land that's free from trouble
　　where there's peace among all men.

Each Spring God Renews His Promise

Long, long ago in a land far away,
There came the dawn of the first Easter Day,
And each year we see the promise reborn
That God gave the world on that first Easter morn.
For in each waking flower and each singing bird
The promise of Easter is witnessed and heard,
And spring is God's way of speaking to men
And renewing the promise of Easter again . . .
For death is a season that man must pass through,
And, just like the flowers, God wakens him, too,
So why should we grieve when our loved ones die,
For we'll meet them again in a cloudless sky.
For Easter is more than a beautiful story—
It's the promise of life and eternal glory.

Lift the Clouds from Your Heart

May Easter wrap its loveliness about your heart,
and may the full significance of the Resurrection
dawn on you as bright and beautiful as the eternal spring.
And whenever dark hours come,
may the remembrance of the Resurrection
shine through the darkness and light your way with faith
and lift the clouds from your heart
as the stone was lifted from the tomb.

The Miracles of Easter

The sleeping earth awakens,
    the robins start to sing—
The flowers open wide their eyes
    to tell us it is spring.
The bleakness of the winter
    is melted by the sun—
The tree that looked so stark and dead
    becomes a living one.
These miracles of Easter,
    wrought with divine perfection,
Are the blessed reassurance
    of our Savior's resurrection.

On the Resurrection Glory

They asked me how I know it's true
    that the Savior lived and died
And if I believe the story
    that the Lord was crucified . . .
And I have so many answers
    to prove His holy being—
Answers that are everywhere
    within the realm of seeing—
The leaves that fall in autumn
    and were buried in the sod
Now budding on the tree boughs
    to lift their arms to God,
The flowers that were covered
    and entombed beneath the snow
Pushing through the darkness
    to bid the spring hello.
On every side, great nature sings
    the Easter story,
So who am I to question
    the Resurrection glory?

An Easter Prayer for Mother

This brings a loving Easter prayer
    that God will truly bless
Your Easter and the springtime
    with peace and happiness . . .
For, Mother, it has always been
    your faith in God above
That filled our home with happiness
    and our hearts with truth and love.

The Joy of Easter Was Born
of Good Friday's Sorrow

Who said the darkness of the night
   would never turn to day?
Who said the winter's bleakness
   would never pass away?
Who said the fog would never lift
   and let the sunshine through?
Who said the skies, now overcast,
   would nevermore be blue?
Why should we ever entertain
   these thoughts so dark and grim
And let the brightness of our minds
   grow cynical and dim
When we know beyond all questioning
   that winter turns to spring
And on the notes of sorrow
   new songs are made to sing?
For no one sheds a teardrop
   or suffers loss in vain,
For God is always there to turn
   our losses into gain . . .
And every burden borne today
   and every present sorrow
Are but God's happy harbingers
   of a joyous, bright tomorrow.

Our Easter Pilgrimage

With our eyes
we see the beauty of Easter,
with our ears
we hear the sounds of spring,
with our hands
we pick the fragrant hyacinths,
with our hearts
we feel the miracle of God's love—
and on the wings of prayer and meditation
we make our Easter pilgrimage to Him.

Commercial Break

Helen wrote poetry and verse from childhood and throughout life for the love of it. But she also made a living from the thousands of pieces she wrote. This section contains just a few of the poems crafted to promote various companies, causes, and projects to which she was devoted.

Helen was barely out of high school before putting her knack for poetry and verse to work for the Ohio Power and Electric Company. She persuaded her supervisor to try promoting their booming electric business in the 1920s with the rhymes she crafted.

The Happiness of Housekeeping

Your room shines out in splendor,
No dirt or dust is seen,
Because the rugs within your house
Are bright and Hoover-clean.

Are You Wired for Today?

Modern babies of modern days
Require things done in modern ways,
And so that each child may have comfort and rest,
We wish to advise the Electric Way's best.
With a Hoover cleaner to catch dust and dirt,
Dear baby can play without being hurt,
For the Hoover will get every germ in the rug
And make baby's playground both comfy and snug.
And then there's a washer to lessen the toil
For mothers who wash all the clothes babies soil;
An ironer to press out the wrinkles and folds,
That baby's adorable little frock holds.
And do not forget baby's bond in this book,
It's something you really should not overlook;
We'll gladly redeem it, for we're trying to say
"Hello, Darling Baby"—the "electric way."

The Realtor's Lament

The lot was grand; the house was fine,
But there was no electric line!
The yard was big and green the grass,
But, oh, alas! There was no gas.
The price was right, a splendid home,
And yet there was no telephone.
It looked supreme when viewed afar,
But who could live with no streetcar!
A house, a lot, a gorgeous place,
But who would sell it in that case,
For who would buy a modern home,
Without electricity, gas, or phone?

Gratitude and Thankfulness

A Thanksgiving Day Prayer

"Faith of our fathers," renew us again
And make us a nation of God-fearing men
Seeking Thy guidance, Thy love, and Thy will,
For we are but pilgrims in search of Thee still . . .
And, gathered together on Thanksgiving Day,
May we lift up our hearts and our hands as we pray
To thank You for blessings we so little merit,
And grant us Thy love and teach us to share it.

Thoughts of Thanks

At this time may God grant you
Special gifts of joy and cheer,
And bless you for the good you do
For others through the year . . .
May you find rich satisfaction
In your daily work and prayer,
And in knowing as you serve Him
He will keep you in His care.

Forever Thanks

Give thanks for the blessings
    that daily are ours—
The warmth of the sun,
    the fragrance of flowers.
With thanks for all the thoughtful,
    caring things you always do
And a loving wish for happiness
    today and all year through!

A Heart Full of Thanksgiving

Everyone needs someone
  to be thankful for,
And each day of life
  we are aware of this more,
For the joy of enjoying
  and the fullness of living
Are found only in hearts
  that are filled with thanksgiving.

My Thanks

People everywhere in life,
  from every walk and station,
From every town and city
  and every state and nation,
Have given me so many things
  intangible and dear
I couldn't begin to count them all
  or even make them clear.
I only know I owe so much
  to people everywhere,
And when I put my thoughts in verse
  it's just a way to share
The musings of a thankful heart,
  a heart much like your own,
For nothing that I think or write
  is mine and mine alone . . .
So if you found some beauty
  in any word or line,
It's just your soul's reflection
  in proximity with mine.

Things to Be Thankful For

The good, green earth beneath our feet,
The air we breathe, the food we eat,
Some work to do, a goal to win,
A hidden longing deep within
That spurs us on to bigger things
And helps us meet what each day brings—
All these things and many more
Are things we should be thankful for . . .
And most of all, our thankful prayers
Should rise to God because He cares.

Words Can Say So Little

Today is an occasion
    for compliments and praise
And saying many of the things
    we don't say other days.
For often through the passing days
    we feel deep down inside
Unspoken thoughts of thankfulness
    and fond, admiring pride.
But words can say so little
    when the heart is overflowing,
And often those we love the most
    just have no way of knowing
The many things the heart conceals
    and never can impart,
For words seem so inadequate
    to express what's in the heart.

Memory Rendezvous

Memory builds a little pathway
    that goes winding through my heart.
It's a lovely, quiet, gentle trail
    from other things apart.
I only meet when traveling there
    the folks I like the best,
For this road I call "remembrance"
    is hidden from the rest,
But I hope I'll always find you
    in my memory rendezvous,
For I keep this little secret place
    to meet with folks like you.

A Thankful Heart

Take nothing for granted, for whenever you do,
The joy of enjoying is lessened for you.
For we rob our own lives much more than we know
When we fail to respond or in any way show
Our thanks for the blessings that daily are ours—
The warmth of the sun, the fragrance of flowers,
The beauty of twilight, the freshness of dawn,
The coolness of dew on a green velvet lawn,
The kind little deeds so thoughtfully done,
The favors of friends and the love that someone
Unselfishly gives us in a myriad of ways,
Expecting no payment and no words of praise.
Oh, great is our loss when we no longer find
A thankful response to things of this kind.
For the joy of enjoying and the fullness of living
Are found in the heart that is filled with thanksgiving.

Thank You, God, for Everything

Thank You, God, for everything—
    the big things and the small—
For every good gift comes from God,
    the Giver of them all,
And all too often we accept
    without any thanks or praise
The gifts God sends as blessings
    each day in many ways.
And so at this time
    we offer up a prayer
To thank You, God, for giving us
    a lot more than our share.
First, thank You for the little things
    that often come our way—
The things we take for granted
    and don't mention when we pray—
The unexpected courtesy,
    the thoughtful, kindly deed,
A hand reached out to help us
    in the time of sudden need.
Oh, make us more aware, dear God,
    of little daily graces
That come to us with sweet surprise
    from never-dreamed-of places.
Then thank You for the miracles
    we are much too blind to see,
And give us new awareness
    of our many gifts from Thee.
And help us to remember
    that the key to life and living
Is to make each prayer a prayer of thanks
    and each day a day of thanksgiving.

So Many Reasons to Love the Lord

Thank You, God, for little things
    that come unexpectedly
To brighten up a dreary day
    that dawned so dismally.
Thank You, God, for sending
    a happy thought my way
To blot out my depression
    on a disappointing day.
Thank You, God, for brushing
    the dark clouds from my mind
And leaving only sunshine
    and joy of heart behind.
Oh, God, the list is endless
    of things to thank You for,
But I take them all for granted
    and unconsciously ignore
That everything I think or do,
    each movement that I make,
Each measured, rhythmic heartbeat,
    each breath of life I take
Is something You have given me
    for which there is no way
For me in all my smallness
    to in any way repay.

The Autumn of Life

What a wonderful time is life's autumn,
　　when the leaves of the trees are all gold,
When God fills each day as He sends it
　　with memories, priceless and old.
What a treasure-house filled with rare jewels
　　are the blessings of year upon year,
When life has been lived as you've lived it
　　in a home where God's presence is near . . .
May the deep meaning surrounding this day,
　　like the paintbrush of God up above,
Touch your life with wonderful blessings.

Be Glad

Be glad that your life has been full and complete,
Be glad that you've tasted the bitter and sweet.
Be glad that you've walked in sunshine and rain,
Be glad that you've felt both pleasure and pain.
Be glad that you've had such a full, happy life,
Be glad for your joy as well as your strife.
Be glad that you've walked with courage each day,
Be glad you've had strength for each step of the way.
Be glad for the comfort that you've found in prayer,
Be glad for God's blessings, His love, and His care.

Keep Us Grateful

Peace dawns once more on a war-torn earth,
While a world gone wild with hysteria and mirth
Raises its voice in loud jubilation
To try to express its heart's exultation.
Cities and towns and country places
Become a seething sea of faces.
Prayers, thanksgiving, and unchecked tears
Mingle with thunderous and unrestrained cheers.
Four days we had lived between war and peace,
Waiting and watching for war to cease,
Now in this hour of triumphal thanksgiving,
We pray for the dead and give thanks for the living.
May we never forget those who sleep 'neath the sod—
They helped liberate, by the grace of our God.
We've reached at long last the victor's goal,
But to keep the peace we must conquer the soul.
We have wrestled and vanquished the enemy,
But we enter a new Gethsemane.
The struggle now enters a realm deep within,
And each man has his own private battle to win . . .
And the words of Christ ring out in our ears
Amid the tumult of victory cheers,
And the Unknown Soldier pleads to be heard,
And his message is told in Christ's stirring words,
"'Ye must be born again,' or we the slain
Have fought and fallen and died in vain."
Keep us grateful, omnipotent God,
And aware of those sleeping beneath the sod.
Strengthen our bonds with one another
So we may dwell as brother to brother.
Heal the wounds and be with us yet,
Lest we forget—lest we forget.

Faith and Perseverance

Never Borrow Sorrow from Tomorrow

Deal only with the present—
    never step into tomorrow,
For God asks us just to trust Him
    and to never borrow sorrow,
For the future is not ours to know,
    and it may never be,
So let us live and give our best
    and give it lavishly . . .
For to meet tomorrow's troubles
    before they are even ours
Is to anticipate the Savior
    and to doubt His all-wise powers,
So let us be content to solve
    our problems one by one,
Asking nothing of tomorrow
    except "Thy will be done."

Mover of Mountains

Faith is a force that is greater
    than knowledge or power or skill,
And the darkest defeat turns to triumph
    if you trust in God's wisdom and will,
For faith is a mover of mountains—
    there's nothing man cannot achieve
If he has the courage to try it
    and then has the faith to believe.

Worry No More—God Knows the Score

Have you ever been caught in a web you didn't weave,
Involved in conditions that are hard to believe?
Have you ever felt you must speak and explain and deny
A story that's groundless or a small, whispered lie?
Have you ever heard rumors you would like to refute
Or some telltale gossip you would like to dispute?
Well, don't be upset, for God knows the score,
And with God as your judge you need worry no more . . .
For men may misjudge you, but God's verdict is fair,
For He looks deep inside and is deeply aware
Of every small detail in your pattern of living,
And always He's fair and lenient and forgiving,
And knowing that God is your judge and your jury
Frees you completely from man's falseness and fury . . .
And, secure in this knowledge, let your thoughts rise above
Man's small, shallow judgments that are so empty of
God's goodness and greatness in judging all men,
And forget ugly rumors and be happy again.

Your Life Will Be Blest If You Look for the Best

It's easy to grow downhearted
    when nothing goes your way,
It's easy to be discouraged
    when you have a troublesome day,
But trouble is only a challenge
    to spur you on to achieve
The best that God has to offer,
    if you have the faith to believe!

Spiritual Lesson from Pain

How little we know what God has in store
As daily He blesses our lives more and more.
I've lived many years and I've learned many things,
But today I have grown new spiritual wings . . .
For pain has a way of broadening our view
And bringing us closer in sympathy, too,
To those who are living in constant pain
And trying somehow to bravely sustain
The faith and endurance to keep on trying
When they almost welcome the peace of dying . . .
Without this experience I would have lived and died
Without fathoming the pain of Christ crucified,
For none of us knows what pain is all about
Until our spiritual wings start to sprout.
So thank You, God, for the gift You sent
To teach me that pain's heaven-sent.

God's Hand Is Always There

I am perplexed and often vexed
And sometimes I cry and sadly sigh,
But do not think, dear Father above,
That I question You or Your unfailing love.
It's just that sometimes when I reach out,
You seem to be nowhere about,
And while I'm sure You love me still
And I know in my heart that You always will,
Somehow I feel I cannot reach You,
And though I get on my knees and beseech You,
I cannot bring You close to me,
And I feel adrift on life's raging sea . . .
But though I cannot find Your hand
To lead me on to the promised land,
I still believe with all my being
Your hand is there beyond my seeing.

"I Am the Light of the World"

In this sick world of hatred
   and violence and sin,
Where society renounces morals
   and rejects discipline,
We stumble in darkness
   groping vainly for light
To distinguish the difference
   between wrong and right . . .
But dawn cannot follow
   this night of despair
Unless faith lights a candle
   in all hearts everywhere . . .
And, warmed by the glow,
   our hate melts away
And love lights the path
   to a peaceful new day.

With God All Things Are Possible

Nothing is ever
   too hard to do
If your faith is strong,
   and your purpose is true . . .
So never give up,
   and never stop—
Just journey on
   to the mountaintop!

A Child's Faith

"Jesus loves me, this I know,
For the Bible tells me so . . ."
Little children ask no more,
For love is all they're looking for,
And in a small child's shining eyes
The faith of all the ages lies . . .
And tiny hands and tousled heads
That kneel in prayer by little beds
Are closer to the dear Lord's heart
And of His kingdom more a part
Than we who search and never find
The answers to our questioning minds—
For faith in things we cannot see
Requires a child's simplicity . . .
For lost in life's complexities,
We drift upon uncharted seas,
And slowly faith disintegrates
While wealth and power accumulate . . .
And the more man learns, the less he knows
And the more involved his thinking grows,
And in his arrogance and pride,
No longer is man satisfied
To place his confidence and love
With childlike faith in God above . . .
Oh, heavenly Father, grant again
A simple, childlike faith to men,
And with a small child's trusting eyes,
May all men come to realize
That faith alone can save man's soul
And lead him to a higher goal.

Patience

Most of the battles
   of life are won
By looking beyond
   the clouds to the sun
And having the patience
   to wait for the day
When the sun comes out
   and the clouds float away.

A Time of Renewal

No one likes to be sick
   and yet we know
It takes sunshine and rain
   to make flowers grow,
And if we never were sick
   and we never felt pain,
We'd be like a desert
   without any rain,
And who wants a life
   that is barren and dry,
With never a cloud
   to darken the sky?
For continuous sun
   goes unrecognized
Like the blessings God sends,
   which are often disguised,
For sometimes a sickness
   that seems so distressing
Is a time of renewal
   and spiritual blessing.

Climb Till Your Dream Comes True

Often your tasks will be many,
    and more than you think you can do.
Often the road will be rugged,
    and the hills insurmountable, too.
But always remember, the hills ahead
    are never as steep as they seem,
And with faith in your heart, start upward
    and climb till you reach your dream.
For nothing in life that is worthy
    is ever too hard to achieve
If you have the courage to try it
    and you have the faith to believe.
For faith is a force that is greater
    than knowledge or power or skill,
And many defeats turn to triumphs
    if you trust in God's wisdom and will.
For faith is a mover of mountains—
    there's nothing that God cannot do—
So start out today with faith in your heart
    and climb till your dream comes true.

God's Sweetest Appointments

Out of life's misery born of man's sins,
A fuller, richer life begins,
For when we are helpless with no place to go
And our hearts are heavy and our spirits are low,
If we place our lives in God's hands
And surrender completely to His will and demands,
The darkness lifts and the sun shines through,
And by His touch we are born anew.
So praise God for trouble that cuts like a knife
And disappointments that shatter your life,

For with patience to wait and faith to endure,
Your life will be blessed and your future secure,
For God is but testing your faith and your love
Before He appoints you to rise far above
All the small things that so sorely distress you,
For God's only intention is to strengthen and bless you.

Faith and Trust

Sometimes when a light
goes out of our lives
and we are left in darkness
and we do not know which way to go,
we must put our hand
into the hand of God
and ask Him to lead us
and if we let our lives become a prayer
until we are strong enough
to stand under the weight
of our own thoughts again,
somehow, even the most difficult
hours are bearable.

Do Not Be Anxious

Do not be anxious, said our Lord,
Have peace from day to day—
The lilies neither toil nor spin,
Yet none are clothed as they.
The meadowlark with sweetest song
Fears not for bread or nest
Because he trusts our Father's love
And God knows what is best.

Never Be Discouraged

There is really nothing we need know
 or even try to understand
If we refuse to be discouraged
 and trust God's guiding hand,
So take heart and meet each minute
 with faith in God's great love,
Aware that every day of life
 is controlled by God above
And never dread tomorrow
 or what the future brings
Just pray for strength and courage
 and trust God in all things,
And never grow discouraged—
 be patient and just wait,
For God never comes too early,
 and He never comes too late.

Trouble Is a Stepping Stone to Growth

Trouble is something no one can escape—
Everyone has it in some form or shape.
Some people hide it way down deep inside,
Some people bear it with gallant-like pride.
Some people worry and complain of their lot,
Some people covet what they haven't got
While others rebel and become bitter and old
With hopes that are dead and hearts that are cold . . .
But the wise man accepts whatever God sends,
Willing to yield like a storm-tossed tree bends,
Knowing that God never made a mistake,
So whatever He sends they are willing to take . . .
For trouble is part and parcel of life,
And no man can grow without struggle or strife,
And the steep hills ahead and the high mountain peaks
Afford man at last the peace that he seeks . . .

So blessed are the people who learn to accept
The trouble men try to escape and reject,
For in accordance we're given great grace
And courage and faith and the strength to face
The daily troubles that come to us all,
So we may learn to stand straight and tall . . .
For the grandeur of life is born of defeat,
For in overcoming we make life complete.

Faith Is a Mighty Fortress

We look ahead through each changing year
With mixed emotions of hope and fear—
Hope for the peace we long have sought,
Fear that our hopes will come to naught.
Unwilling to trust in the Father's will,
We count on our logic and shallow skill,
And in our arrogance and pride,
We are no longer satisfied
To place our confidence and love
With childlike faith in God above.
And tiny hands and tousled heads
That kneel in prayer by little beds
Are closer to the dear Lord's heart
And of His kingdom more a part
Than we who search and never find
The answers to our questioning minds—
For faith in things we cannot see
Requires a child's simplicity.
Oh, heavenly Father, grant again
A simple, childlike faith to men,
Forgetting color, race, and creed
And seeing only the heart's deep need.
For faith alone can save man's soul
And lead him to a higher goal,
For there's but one unfailing course—
We win by faith and not by force.

He Asks So Little and Gives So Much

What must I do to ensure peace of mind?
Is the answer I'm seeking too hard to find?
How can I know what God wants me to be?
How can I tell what's expected of me?
Where can I go for guidance and aid
To help me correct the errors I've made?
The answer is found in doing three things,
And great is the gladness that doing them brings.
"Do justice"—"Love kindness"—"Walk humbly with
    God"—
For with these three things as your rule and your rod,
All things worth having are yours to achieve,
If you follow God's words and have faith to believe.

Faith for Dark Days

When dark days come—and they come to us all—
We feel so helpless and lost and small.
We cannot fathom the reason why,
And it is futile for us to try
To find the answer, the reason or cause,
For the master plan is without any flaws . . .
And when the darkness shuts out the light,
We must lean on faith to restore our sight,
For there is nothing we need know
If we have faith that wherever we go
God will be there to help us to bear
Our disappointments, pain, and care,
For He is our Shepherd, our Father, our Guide,
And you're never alone with the Lord at your side . . .
So may the great Physician attend you,
And may His healing completely mend you.

Faith Alone

When the way seems long and the day is dark
And we can't hear the sound of the thrush or the lark
And our hearts are heavy with worry and care
And we are lost in the depths of despair,
That is the time when faith alone
Can lead us out of the dark unknown . . .
For faith to believe when the way is rough
And faith to hang on when the going is tough
Will never fail to pull us through
And bring us strength and comfort, too . . .
For all we really ever need
Is faith as a grain of mustard seed,
For all God asks is Do you believe?
For if you do ye shall receive.

Trust God

Take heart and meet each minute
        with faith in God's great love,
Aware that every day of life
        is controlled by God above . . .
And never dread tomorrow
        or what the future brings—
Just pray for strength and courage
        and trust God in all things.

Anxious Prayers

When we are deeply disturbed by a problem
    and our minds are filled with doubt,
And we struggle to find a solution
    but there seems to be no way out,
We futilely keep on trying
    to untangle our web of distress,
But our own little, puny efforts
    meet with very little success.
And finally, exhausted and weary,
    discouraged and downcast and low,
With no foreseeable answer
    and with no other place to go,
We kneel down in sheer desperation
    and slowly and stumblingly pray,
Then impatiently wait for an answer
    in one sudden instant, we say,
"God does not seem to be listening,
    so why should we bother to pray?"
But God can't get through to the anxious,
    who are much too impatient to wait,
You have to believe in God's promise
    that He comes not too soon or too late,
For whether God answers promptly
    or delays in answering your prayer,
You must have faith to believe Him
    and to know in your heart He'll be there.
So be not impatient or hasty,
    just trust in the Lord and believe,
For whatever you ask in faith and love,
    in abundance you are sure to receive.

Burdens Can Be Blessings

Our Father knows what's best for us,
So why should we complain—
We always want the sunshine,
But He knows there must be rain—
We love the sound of laughter
And the merriment of cheer,
But our hearts would lose their tenderness
If we never shed a tear . . .
So whenever we are troubled
And life has lost its song
It's God testing us with burdens
Just to make our spirit strong!

Expectation! Anticipation! Realization!

God gives us a power we so seldom employ
For we're so unaware it is filled with such joy.
The gift that God gives us is anticipation,
Which we can fulfill with sincere expectation,
For there's power in belief when we think we will find
Joy for the heart and peace for the mind,
And believing the day will bring a surprise
Is not only pleasant but surprisingly wise . . .
For we open the door to let joy walk through
When we learn to expect the best and most, too,
And believing we'll find a happy surprise
Makes reality out of a fancied surmise.

Adversity Can Bless Us

The way we use adversity
    is strictly our own choice,
For in God's hands
    adversity can make the heart rejoice.
For everything God sends to us,
    no matter in what form,
Is sent with plan and purpose,
    for by the fierceness of a storm
The atmosphere is changed and cleared
    and the earth is washed and clean,
And the high winds of adversity
    can make restless souls serene.
And while it's very difficult
    for mankind to understand
God's intentions and His purpose
    and the workings of His hand,
If we observe the miracles
    that happen every day,
We cannot help but be convinced
    that in His wondrous way
God makes what seemed unbearable
    and painful and distressing
Easily acceptable
    when we view it as a blessing.

Great Faith That Smiles Is Born of Trials

It's easy to say "In God we trust"
    when life is radiant and fair,
But the test of faith is only found
    when there are burdens to bear . . .
For our claim to faith in the sunshine
    is really no faith at all,
For when roads are smooth and days are bright
    our need for God is so small . . .

And no one discovers the fullness
    or the greatness of God's love
Unless they have walked in the darkness
    with only a light from above . . .
For the faith to endure whatever comes
    is born of sorrow and trials
And strengthened only by discipline
    and nurtured by self-denials . . .
So be not disheartened by troubles,
    for trials are the building blocks
On which to erect a fortress of faith,
    secure on God's ageless rocks.

The End of the Road Is But a Bend in the Road

When we feel we have nothing left to give
    and we are sure that the song has ended,
When our day seems over and the shadows fall
    and the darkness of night has descended,
Where can we go to find the strength
    to valiantly keep on trying?
Where can we find the hand that will dry
    the tears that the heart is crying?
There's but one place to go and that is to God,
    and, dropping all pretense and pride,
We can pour out our problems without restraint
    and gain strength with Him at our side . . .
And together we stand at life's crossroads
    and view what we think is the end,
But God has a much bigger vision,
    and He tells us it's only a bend . . .
For the road goes on and is smoother,
    and the pause in the song is a rest,
And the part that's unsung and unfinished
    is the sweetest and richest and best . . .
So rest and relax and grow stronger—
    let go and let God share your load.
Your work is not finished or ended—
    you've just come to a bend in the road.

We Can't, but God Can

Why things happen as they do
   we do not always know,
And we cannot always fathom
   why our spirits sink so low.
We flounder in our dark distress,
   we are wavering and unstable,
But when we're most inadequate,
   The Lord God's always able—
For though we are incapable,
   God's powerful and great,
And there's no darkness of the mind
   God cannot penetrate . . .
And all that is required of us
   whenever things go wrong
Is to trust in God implicitly
   with a faith that's deep and strong . . .
And while He may not instantly
   unravel all the strands
Of the tangled thoughts that trouble us,
   He completely understands—
And in His time, if we have faith,
   He will gradually restore
The brightness to our spirits
   that we've been longing for . . .
So remember there's no cloud too dark
   for God's light to penetrate
If we keep on believing
   and have faith enough to wait.

Encouragement, Comfort, and Hope

The Comfort and Sweetness of Peace

After the clouds, the sunshine,
After the winter, the spring,
After the shower, the rainbow—
For life is a changeable thing,
After the night, the morning
Bidding all darkness cease,
After life's cares and sorrows,
The comfort and sweetness of peace.

There Are Blessings in Everything

Blessings come in many guises
That God alone in love devises,
And sickness, which we dread so much,
Can bring a very healing touch,
For often on the wings of pain
The peace we sought before in vain
Will come to us with sweet surprise,
For God is merciful and wise . . .
And through long hours of tribulation
God gives us time for meditation,
And no sickness can be counted loss
That teaches us to bear our cross.

How Great the Yield from a Fertile Field

The farmer plows through the fields of green,
And the blade of the plow is sharp and keen,
But the seed must be sown to bring forth grain,
For nothing is born without suffering and pain,
And God never plows in the soul of man
Without intention and purpose and plan . . .
So whenever you feel the plow's sharp blade

Let not your heart be sorely afraid,
For, like the farmer, God chooses a field
From which He expects an excellent yield . . .
So rejoice though your heart be broken in two—
God seeks to bring forth a rich harvest in you.

A Meditation

God in His loving and all-wise way
Makes the heart that once was so young yesterday
Serene and more gentle and less restless, too,
Content to remember the joys it once knew . . .
And all that we sought on the pathway of pleasure
Becomes but a memory to cherish and treasure—
The fast pace grows slower and the spirit serene,
And the soul can envision what the eyes have not seen . . .
And so while life's springtime is sweet to recall,
The autumn of life is the best time of all,
For our wild youthful yearnings all gradually cease
And God fills our days with beauty and peace!

A New Beginning

It doesn't take a new year
    to begin our lives anew—
God grants us new beginnings
    each day the whole year through.
So never be discouraged,
    for there comes daily to all men
The chance to make another start
    and begin all over again.

This Too Will Pass Away

If I can endure for this minute
    whatever is happening to me
No matter how heavy my heart is
    or how dark the moment might be—
If I can remain calm and quiet
    with all my world crashing about me,
Secure in the knowledge God loves me
    when everyone else seems to doubt me—
If I can but keep on believing
    what I know in my heart to be true,
That darkness will fade with the morning
    and that this will pass away, too—
Then nothing in life can defeat me,
    for, as long as this knowledge remains,
I can suffer whatever is happening,
    for I know God will break all the chains
That are binding me tight in the darkness
    and trying to fill me with fear . . .
For there is no night without dawning,
    and I know that my morning is near.

Give Me the Contentment of Acceptance

In the deep, dark hours of my distress,
My unworthy life seems a miserable mess.
Handicapped, limited, with my strength decreasing,
The demands on my time keep forever increasing,
And I pray for the flair and the force of youth
So I can keep spreading God's light and His truth,
For my heart's happy hope and my dearest desire
Is to continue to serve You with fervor and fire,
But I no longer have strength to dramatically do
The spectacular things I loved doing for You,

Forgetting entirely that all You required
Was not a servant the world admired
But a humbled heart and a sanctified soul
Whose only mission and purpose and goal
Was to be content with whatever God sends
And to know that to please You really depends
Not on continued and mounting success
But on learning how to become less and less
And to realize that we serve God best
When our one desire and only request
Is not to succumb to worldly acclaim
But to honor ourselves in Your holy name.
So let me say no to the flattery and praise
And quietly spend the rest of my days
Far from the greed and the speed of man,
Who has so distorted God's simple life plan,
And let me be great in the eyes of You, Lord,
For that is the richest, most priceless reward.

A Message of Consolation

On the wings of death and sorrow
God sends us new hope for tomorrow,
And in His mercy and His grace
He gives us strength to bravely face
The lonely days that stretch ahead
And to know our loved one is not dead
But only sleeping out of our sight,
And we'll meet in that land where there is no night.

When Trouble Comes and Things Go Wrong

Let us go quietly to God
    when troubles come to us.
Let us never stop to whimper
    or complain or fret or fuss.
Let us hide our thorns in roses
    and our sighs in golden song
And our crosses in a crown of smiles
    whenever things go wrong . . .
For no one can really help us
    as our troubles we bemoan,
For comfort, help, and inner peace
    must come from God alone . . .
So do not tell your neighbor,
    your companion, or your friend
In the hope that they can help you
    bring your troubles to an end,
For they too have their problems—
    they are burdened just like you—
So take your cross to Jesus,
    and He will see you through . . .
And waste no time in crying
    on the shoulder of a friend,
But go directly to the Lord,
    for on Him you can depend . . .
For there's absolutely nothing
    that His mighty hand can't do,
And He never is too busy
    to help and comfort you.

Warm Our Hearts with Thy Love

Oh, God, who made the summer
   and warmed the earth with beauty,
Warm our hearts with gratitude
   and devotion to our duty . . .
For in this age of violence,
   rebellion and defiance,
We've forgotten the true meaning
   of dependable reliance.
We have lost our sense of duty
   and our sense of values, too,
And what was once unsanctioned
   no longer is taboo.
Our standards have been lowered,
   and we resist all discipline,
And our vision has been narrowed
   and blinded to all sin.
Oh, put the summer brightness
   in our closed, unseeing eyes
So in the careworn faces
   that we pass we'll recognize
The heartbreak and the loneliness,
   the trouble and despair
That a word of understanding
   would make easier to bear.
Oh, God, look down on our cold hearts
   and warm them with Your love,
And grant us Your forgiveness
   which we're so unworthy of.

Dark Shadows Fall in the Lives of Us All

Sickness and sorrow come to us all,
But through it we grow and learn to stand tall—
For trouble is part and parcel of life,
And no man can grow without struggle and strife.
The more we endure with patience and grace,
The stronger we grow and the more we can face—
And the more we can face, the greater our love,
And with love in our hearts we are more conscious of
The pain and the sorrow in lives everywhere—
So it is through trouble that we learn to share.

Life's Crossroads

Sometimes we come to life's crossroads
    and view what we think is the end,
But God has a much wider vision,
    and He knows it's only a bend—
The road will go on and get smoother,
    and after we've stopped for a rest,
The path that lies hidden beyond us
    is often the part that is best . . .
So rest and relax and grow stronger—
    let go and let God share your load,
And have faith in a brighter tomorrow—
    you've just come to a bend in the road.

Discouragement and Dreams

So many things in the line of duty
Drain us of effort and leave us no beauty,
And the dust of the soul grows thick and unswept,
The spirit is drenched in tears unwept.
But just as we fall beside the road,
Discouraged with life and bowed down with our load,
We lift our eyes, and what seemed a dead end
Is the street of dreams where we meet a friend.

Blessings Come in Many Guises

When troubles come and things go wrong
And days are cheerless and nights are long,
We find it so easy to give in to despair
By magnifying the burdens we bear.
We add to our worries by refusing to try
To look for the rainbow in an overcast sky,
And the blessings God sent in a darkened disguise
Our troubled hearts fail to recognize,
Not knowing God sent it not to distress us
But to strengthen our faith and redeem us and bless us.

A Loving Wish for a Happy Day

A wish that's sent with lots of love
Just seems to have a feeling—
A special word or sentiment
That makes it more appealing,
And that's the kind of loving wish
That's being sent your way
To hope that every day will be
Your happy kind of day.

Never Despair, God's Always There

In sickness or health,
In suffering and pain,
In storm-laden skies,
In sunshine and rain,
God always is there
To lighten your way
And lead you through darkness
To a much brighter day.

This Is Just a Resting Place

Sometimes the road of life seems long
    as we travel through the years
And, with a heart that's broken
    and eyes brimful of tears,
We falter in our weariness
    and sink beside the way,
But God leans down and whispers,
    "Child, there'll be another day,"
And the road will grow much smoother
    and much easier to face,
So do not be disheartened—
    this is just a resting place.

A Tribute to John F. Kennedy

His gallant soul has but taken flight
Into the land where there is no night.
He is not dead, he has only gone on
Into a brighter and more wonderful dawn.
For his passion for justice among men of goodwill
No violence can silence, no bullet can still.
For his spirit lives on and, like the warm sun,
It will nourish the dreams that he had begun.
So this hour of sorrow is only God's will,

For the good in this man is living here still . . .
Forgive our transgressions and revive us anew
So we may draw closer to each other and You.
For unless "God is guard," John Kennedy said,
"We're standing unguarded," with dreams that are dead.
For a nation too proud to kneel down and pray
Will crumble to chaos and descend to decay.
So use what He gave for a rededication
And make this once more a God-fearing nation—
A symbol of hope and a standard for good
As we lead in the struggle for a new brotherhood!

Written over a weekend at the request of Lawrence Welk. It was read on
Lawrence Welk's television program in tribute to the assassinated presi-
dent. The reading was rebroadcast many times upon public request.

Lives Distressed Cannot Be Blessed

Refuse to be discouraged—
    refuse to be distressed,
For when we are despondent,
    our lives cannot be blessed,
For doubt and fear and worry
    close the door to faith and prayer,
And there's no room for blessings
    when we're lost in deep despair.
So remember when you're troubled
    with uncertainty and doubt,
It is best to tell our Father
    what our fear is all about,
For unless we seek His guidance
    when troubled times arise,
We are bound to make decisions
    that are twisted and unwise,
But when we view our problems
    through the eyes of God above,
Misfortunes turn to blessings
    and hatred turns to love.

In Hours of Discouragement, God Is Our Encouragement

Sometimes we feel uncertain
    and unsure of everything—
Afraid to make decisions,
    dreading what the day will bring.
We keep wishing it were possible
    to dispel all fear and doubt
And to understand more readily
    just what life is all about.
God has given us the answers,
    which too often go unheeded,
But if we search His promises
    we'll find everything that's needed
To lift our faltering spirits
    and renew our courage, too,
For there's absolutely nothing
    too much for God to do . . .
For the Lord is our salvation
    and our strength in every fight,
Our redeemer and protector,
    our eternal guiding light.
He has promised to sustain us,
    He's our refuge from all harms,
And underneath this refuge
    are the everlasting arms . . .
So cast your burden on Him,
    seek His counsel when distressed,
And go to Him for comfort
    when you're lonely and oppressed . . .
For in God is our encouragement
    in trouble and in trials,
And in suffering and in sorrow
    He will turn our tears to smiles.

The Seasons of the Soul

Why am I cast down and despondently sad
When I long to be happy and joyous and glad?
Why is my heart heavy with unbearable weight
As I try to escape this soul-saddened state?
I ask myself often what makes life this way—
Why is the song silenced in my heart today?
And then with God's help it all becomes clear—
The soul has its seasons just the same as the year.
I too must pass through life's autumn of dying,
A desolate period of heart-hurt and crying,
Followed by winter, in whose frostbitten hand
My heart is as frozen as the snow-covered land.
We too must pass through the seasons God sends,
Content in the knowledge that everything ends.

Be of Good Cheer, There's Nothing to Fear

Cheerful thoughts like sunbeams lighten up the darkest fears,
For when the heart is happy there's just no time for tears,
And when the face is smiling it's impossible to frown,
And when you are high-spirited you cannot feel low-down . . .
For the nature of our attitudes toward circumstantial things
Determines our acceptance of the problems that life brings,
And since fear and dread and worry cannot help in any way,
It's much healthier and happier to be cheerful every day . . .
And if you'll only try it, you will find, without a doubt,
A cheerful attitude's something no one should be without,
For when the heart is cheerful, it cannot be filled with fear,
And without fear, the way ahead seems more distinct and clear,
And we realize there's nothing that we must face alone,
For our heavenly Father loves us, and our problems are His own.

A Word of Understanding

May peace and understanding
Give you strength and courage, too,
And may the hours and days ahead
Hold a new hope for you;
For the sorrow that is yours today
Will pass away and then
You'll find the sun of happiness
Will shine for you again.

The Way to God

If my days were untroubled and my heart always light,
Would I seek that fair land where there is no night?
If I never grew weary with the weight of my load,
Would I search for God's peace at the end of the road?
If I never knew sickness and never felt pain,
Would I reach for a hand to help and sustain?
If I walked not with sorrow and lived not with loss,
Would my soul seek sweet solace at the foot of the cross?
If all I desired was mine day by day,
Would I kneel before God and earnestly pray?
If God sent no winter to freeze me with fear,
Would I yearn for the warmth of spring every year?
I ask myself this and the answer is plain—
If my life were all pleasure and I never knew pain,
I'd seek God less often and need Him much less,
For God's sought more often in times of distress—
And no one knows God or sees Him as plain
As those who have met Him on the pathway of pain.

Wish Not for Ease or to Do as You Please

If wishes worked like magic and plans worked that way, too,
And if everything you wished for, whether good or bad for you,
Immediately were granted with no effort on your part,
You'd experience no fulfillment of your spirit or your heart . . .
For things achieved too easily lose their charm and meaning, too,
For it is life's difficulties and the trial times we go through
That make us strong in spirit and endow us with the will
To surmount the insurmountable and to climb the highest hill . . .
So wish not for the easy way to win your heart's desire,
For the joy's in overcoming and withstanding flood and fire,
For to triumph over trouble and grow stronger with defeat
Is to win the kind of victory that will make your life complete.

Meet Life's Trials with Smiles

There are times when life overwhelms us
    and our trials seem too many to bear—
It is then we should stop to remember
    God is standing by ready to share
The uncertain hours that confront us
    and fill us with fear and despair,
For God in His goodness has promised
    that the cross that He gives us to wear
Will never exceed our endurance
    or be more than our strength can bear . . .
And secure in that blessed assurance,
    we can smile as we face tomorrow,
For God holds the key to the future,
    and no sorrow or care we need borrow.

Before You Can Dry Another's Tears,
You Too Must Weep

Let me not live a life that's free
From the things that draw me close to Thee,
For how can I ever hope to heal
The wounds of others I do not feel?
If my eyes are dry and I never weep,
How do I know when the hurt is deep?
If my heart is cold and it never bleeds,
How can I tell what my brother needs?
For when ears are deaf to the beggar's plea
And we close our eyes and refuse to see
And we steel our hearts and harden our minds
And we count it a weakness whenever we're kind,
We are no longer following the Father's way
Or seeking His guidance from day to day . . .
For, without crosses to carry and burdens to bear,
We dance through a life that is frothy and fair,
And, chasing the rainbow, we have no desire
For roads that are rough and realms that are higher . . .
So spare me no heartache or sorrow, dear Lord,
For the heart that hurts reaps the richest reward,
And God blesses the heart that is broken with sorrow
As He opens the door to a brighter tomorrow . . .
For only through tears can we recognize
The suffering that lies in another's eyes.

Look on the Sunny Side

There are always two sides—
    the good and the bad,
The dark and the light,
    the sad and the glad . . .
But in looking back over
    the good and the bad,
We're aware of the number
    of good things we've had—
And in counting our blessings,
    we find when we're through
We've no reason at all
    to complain or be blue . . .
So thank God for the good things
    He has already done,
And be grateful to Him
    for the battles you've won—
And know that the same God
    who helped you before
Is ready and willing
    to help you once more—
Then with faith in your heart,
    reach out for God's hand
And accept what He sends,
    though you can't understand . . .
For our Father in heaven
    always knows what is best,
And if you trust His wisdom,
    your life will be blessed . . .
For always remember
    that, whatever betide you,
You are never alone,
    for God is beside you.

You're Never Alone

There's truly nothing
    we need know
If we have faith
    wherever we go,
God will be there
    to help us bear
Our disappointments,
    pain and care,
For He is our Shepherd,
    our Father, our Guide—
You're never alone
    with the Lord at your side.

Only God

At times like these
man is helpless . . .
it is only God
who can speak the words
that calm the sea,
still the wind,
and ease the pain . . .
so lean on Him
and you will never walk alone.

The Comfort of Transformation

If we never suffered tragedy and we never felt sorrow, how could our souls grow? In my husband's tragic death, which was so hurried and unscheduled, it was difficult for me, when I was very young, to see what the purpose could have been. But now I know that he sacrificed his life that my life might be lived in a fuller and richer way, for his sudden death transformed my entire life. I could never have done what I am doing now if I had not felt the pangs of sorrow, for you cannot dry the tears of those who weep unless you have cried yourself.

I know, when death comes flashing out of a bright sky suddenly and unexpectedly in the midst of youthful enjoyment when life is flushed with hope and filled with dreams, it is very, very difficult to accept God's judgment. It is hard to reconcile ourselves to such a loss when God asks us to give up someone young and in mid-career with abundant years stretching ahead of them, for to have a life so suddenly silenced is beyond our understanding. But there is something brave and beautiful in passing at this high peak, while standing on tiptoe, into new fields of usefulness. And you must realize, dear, that he just rose unencumbered to meet God, and he is safe and free where all the problems of this restless, violent world will no longer disturb his young mind.

May God comfort you and show you the way. But remember, God does not comfort us to make us more comfortable. He comforts us so that we may also become comforters.

Words say so little when the heart means so much.

Giving and Service

Life

If you would aspire a salesman to be
The rulings are simple and few—
Just work, be happy, and never forget
You're paid for whatever you do.
If you bargain with life for a penny,
You'll find life will pay you no more,
And you'll feel that you've failed completely
When you figure your final score.
If you realize life's an employer
That pays you whatever you ask
You'll learn to be honest and never deceive
In any performance or task.
So just set your wage at the highest stake,
And never give up in dismay,
For any wage you may ask of Life,
Old Life will so gladly pay.

This verse, located in the Helen Steiner Rice Foundation archives, is
from a speech Helen gave in the 1920s and always liked.

His Footsteps

When someone does a kindness,
It always seems to me
That's the way God up in heaven
Would like us all to be.
For when we bring some pleasure
To another human heart,
We have followed in His footsteps
And we've had a little part
In serving God who loves us—
For I'm very sure it's true
That in serving those around us,
We serve and please God, too.

Heart Gifts

It's not the things that can be bought
That are life's richest treasures,
It's just the little "heart gifts"
That money cannot measure—
A cheerful smile, a friendly word,
A sympathetic nod,
All priceless little treasures
From the storehouse of our God—
They are the things that can't be bought
With silver or with gold,
For thoughtfulness and kindness
And love are never sold—
They are the priceless things in life
For which no one can pay,
And the giver finds rich recompense
In giving them away.

Serving Your Land by Hand

You've been asked to join the Army,
You've been asked to join a lodge,
You've been asked to join a party,
And perhaps you've tried to dodge;
But now it is the *Red Cross*,
That asks you for your name
And surely you will join the ranks
That stand for *Service* fame.
It only costs a dollar
To be rated with the rest,
And when you join the *Red Cross*,
You've selected quite the best.
Your dollar keeps on working
Through this "mighty human hand,"
And you have the satisfaction
Of helping SERVE your land!

As chairperson of publicity and advertising for her hometown's
American Red Cross drive, Helen Steiner wrote this verse, which
appeared in the local newspaper in 1925.

Business

This is more than a way to earn your pay,
More than a place to report each day.
It's part of your life, and the hours spent here
Comprise a big share of your living each year,
And that is the reason you never should feel
That you're just a number or a cog in a wheel.
We are part of a team and a circle of friends
Reaching beyond where our own job ends,
Not standing alone but a part of a whole
Striving together for one common goal.
What person can boast, "I won on my own,"
Or truthfully say, "I did this alone,"
When everyone holding a job great or small
Contributes a part to the future of all!

Written by Helen E. Steiner for use in speaking engagements.

The World Would Be a Nicer Place
If We Traveled at a Slower Pace

Amid stresses and strains,
     much too many to mention,
And pressure-packed days
     filled with turmoil and tension,
We seldom have time
     to be friendly or kind,
For we're harassed and hurried
     and always behind . . .
And while we've more gadgets
     and buttons to press
Making leisure time greater
     and laboring less

And our standards of living
    they claim have improved
And repressed inhibitions
    have been freed and removed,
It seems all this progress
    and growth are for naught,
For daily we see
    a world more distraught . . .
So what does it matter
    if man reaches his goal
And gains the whole world
    but loses his soul?
For what have we won
    if in gaining this end
We've been much too busy
    to be kind to a friend?
And what is there left
    to make the heart sing
When life is a cold
    and mechanical thing?
And are we but puppets
    of controlled automation
Instead of joint heirs
    to God's gift of creation?

The Story of Albrecht Dürer

As you read this poem, perhaps you'd like to know
That this story really happened many centuries ago
When two talented young artists were struggling hard to earn
Just enough to live on so both of them might learn
How to be great artists and leave behind a name
That many centuries later would still retain its fame.
But in their dire necessity for the warmth of food and fire,
One of the artists sacrificed his dream and heart's desire
So he might earn a living and provide enough to eat
Till both of them were back again securely on their feet.
But months and years of grueling toil destroyed the craftsman's touch,
And scarred and stiffened were the hands that held promise of so much.
He could no longer hold a brush the way he used to do,
And the dream he once had cherished no longer could come true.
So uncomplainingly he lived with his friend, who had succeeded
And now could purchase all the things they once had so much needed.
But the famous Albrecht Dürer, the friend we're speaking of,
Was always conscious that he owed a debt of thanks and love
To one who sacrificed his skill so that Dürer might succeed.
But how can anyone repay a sacrificial deed?
Then, when he saw those hands in prayer, he decided he would paint
A picture for the world to see of this unheralded saint.
So down through countless ages and in many, many lands,
All men could see the beauty in these toilworn praying hands,
And seeing, they would recognize that behind fame and success
Somebody sacrificed a dream for another's happiness.

The Praying Hands

"The Praying Hands" is much, much more than just a work of art—
It is the soul's creation of a deeply thankful heart.
It is a priceless masterpiece that love alone could paint,
And it reveals the selflessness of an unheralded saint.
These hands, so scarred and toilworn, tell the story of a man
Who sacrificed his talent in accordance with God's plan,
And in God's plan are many things man cannot understand,
But we must trust God's judgment and be guided by His hand.
Sometimes He asks us to give up our dreams of happiness—
Sometimes we must forego our hopes of fortune and success.
Not all of us can triumph or rise to heights of fame,
And many times what should be ours goes to another name,
But he who makes a sacrifice so another may succeed
Is indeed a true disciple of our blessed Savior's creed,
For when we give ourselves away in sacrifice and love,
We are laying up rich treasures in God's kingdom up above.
And hidden in gnarled, toilworn hands is the truest art of living,
Achieved alone by those who've learned the victory of giving,
For any sacrifice on earth made in the dear Lord's name
Assures the giver of a place in heaven's hall of fame.
And who can say with certainty where the greatest talent lies
Or who will be the greatest in our heavenly Father's eyes?
And who can tell with certainty, in the heavenly Father's sight,
Who's entitled to the medals and who's the hero of the fight?

Giving Is the Key to Living

Every day is a reason for giving
And giving is the key to living . . .
So let us give ourselves away,
Not just today but every day,
And remember, a kind and thoughtful deed
Or a hand outstretched in a time of need
Is the rarest of gifts, for it is a part
Not of the purse but a loving heart . . .
And he who gives of himself will find
True joy of heart and peace of mind.

The Richness in Kindness

It's not fortune or fame
    or worldwide acclaim
That makes for true greatness,
    you'll find—
It's the wonderful art
    of teaching the heart
To always be thoughtful and kind!

Traveling to Heaven

Life is a highway
    on which the years go by,
Sometimes the road is level,
    sometimes the hills are high . . .
But as we travel onward
    to a future that's unknown,
We can make each mile we travel
    a heavenly stepping stone!

Make Me a Channel of Blessing Today

Make me a channel of blessing today—
    I ask again and again when I pray.
Do I turn a deaf ear to the Master's voice
    or refuse to hear His directions and choice?
I only know at the end of the day
    that I did so little to pay my way.

Give Lavishly! Live Abundantly!

The more you give,
    the more you get—
The more you laugh,
    the less you fret.
The more you do
    unselfishly,
The more you live
    abundantly—
The more of everything
    you share,
The more you'll always
    have to spare.
The more you love,
    the more you'll find
That life is good
    and friends are kind,
For only what
    we give away
Enriches us
    from day to day.

Slowing Down

My days are so crowded and my hours so few
And I can no longer work fast like I used to do.
But I know I must learn to be satisfied,
That God has not completely denied
The joy of working—at a much slower pace—
For as long as he gives me a little place
To work with Him in His vineyard of love,
Just to know that He's helping me from above
Gives me strength to meet each day
As I travel along life's changing way.

The Blessing of Sharing

Only what we give away
Enriches us from day to day,
For not in getting but in giving
Is found the lasting joy of living,
For no one ever had a part
In sharing treasures of the heart
Who did not feel the impact of
The magic mystery of God's love.
Love alone can make us kind
And give us joy and peace of mind,
So live with joy unselfishly
And you'll be blessed abundantly.

Teach Me

Teach me to give of myself
   in whatever way I can,
   of whatever I have to give.
Teach me to value myself—
   my time, my talents,
   my purpose, my life,
   my meaning in Your world.

The Fragrance Remains

There's an old Chinese proverb
   that if practiced each day
Would change the whole world
   in a wonderful way.
Its truth is so simple,
   it's easy to do,
And it works every time
   and successfully, too.
For you can't do a kindness
   without a reward—
Not in silver nor gold
   but in joy from the Lord.
You can't light a candle
   to show others the way
Without feeling the warmth
   of that bright little ray,
And you can't pluck a rose
   all fragrant with dew
Without part of its fragrance
   remaining with you.

God-Given Drive

There's a difference between drive and driven,
The one is selfish, the other God-given,
For the driven man has but one goal—
Just worldly wealth and not riches of soul . . .
And daily he's spurred on to reach and attain
A higher position, more profit and gain.
Ambition and wealth become his great needs
As daily he's driven by avarice and greed . . .
But most blessed are they who use their drive
To work with zeal so all men may survive,
For while they forfeit great personal gain,
Their work and their zeal are never in vain
For they contribute to the whole human race,
And we cannot survive without growing in grace . . .
So help us, dear God, to choose between
The driving forces that rule our routine
So we may make our purpose and goal
Not power and wealth but the growth of our souls . . .
And give us strength and drive and desire
To raise our standards and ethics higher,
So all of us and not just a few
May live on earth as You want us to.

A Gift of Love

Time is not measured by the years that you live
But by the deeds that you do and the joy that you give . . .
And from birthday to birthday, the good Lord above
Bestows on His children the gift of His love,
Asking us only to share it with others
By treating all people not as strangers but brothers . . .
And each day as it comes brings a chance to each one
To live to the fullest, leaving nothing undone

That would brighten the life or lighten the load
Of some weary traveler lost on life's road . . .
So what does it matter how long we may live
If as long as we live we unselfishly give.

Take Time to Be Kind

Kindness is a virtue
  given by the Lord—
It pays dividends in happiness
  and joy is its reward.
For if you practice kindness
  in all you say and do,
The Lord will wrap His kindness
  around your heart and you.

It's a Wonderful World

In spite of the fact we complain and lament
And view this old world with much discontent,
Deploring conditions and grumbling because
There's so much injustice and so many flaws,
It's a wonderful world, and it's people like you
Who make it that way by the things that they do.
For a warm, ready smile or a kind, thoughtful deed
Or a hand outstretched in an hour of need
Can change our whole outlook and make the world bright
Where a minute before just nothing seemed right.
It's a wonderful world and it always will be
If we keep our eyes open and focused to see
The wonderful things we are capable of
When we open our hearts to God and His love.

Count Your Gains, Not Losses

As we travel down life's busy road
Complaining of our heavy load,
We often think God's been unfair
And gave us much more than our share
Of daily little irritations
And disappointing tribulations.
We're discontented with our lot
And all the bad breaks that we got.
We count our losses not our gain,
And remember only tears and pain.
The good things we forget completely—
When God looked down and blessed us sweetly.
Our troubles fill our every thought—
We dwell upon the goals we sought,
And, wrapped up in our own despair,
We have no time to see or share
Another's load that far outweighs
Our little problems and dismays . . .
And so we walk with heads held low,
And little do we guess or know
That someone near us on life's street
Is burdened deeply with defeat,
And if we'd but forget our care
And stop in sympathy to share
The burden that our brother carried,
Our minds and hearts would be less harried
And we would feel our load was small—
In fact, we carried no load at all.

The World Needs Friendly Folks like You

In this troubled world
    it's refreshing to find
Someone who still
    has the time to be kind,
Someone who still
    has the faith to believe
That the more that you give,
    the more you receive,
Someone who's ready
    by thought, word, or deed
To reach out a hand
    in the hour of need.

Brighten the Corner Where You Are

We cannot all be famous or listed in "Who's Who,"
But every person, great or small, has important work to do . . .
For seldom do we realize the importance of small deeds
Or to what degree of greatness unnoticed kindness leads . . .
For it's not the big celebrity in a world of fame and praise,
But it's doing unpretentiously in indistinguished ways
The work that God assigned to us, unimportant as it seems,
That makes our task outstanding and brings reality to dreams . . .
So do not sit and idly wish for wider, new dimensions
Where you can put in practice your many good intentions,
But at the spot God placed you, begin at once to do
Little things to brighten up the lives surrounding you . . .
For if everybody brightened up the spot on which they're standing
By being more considerate and a little less demanding,
This dark old world would very soon eclipse the evening star,
If everybody brightened up the corner where they are.

God's Care
and Provision

Stepping Stones to God

An aching heart is but a stepping stone
To greater joy than you've ever known,
For things that cause the heart to ache
Until you think that it must break
Become the strength by which we climb
To higher heights that are sublime
And feel the radiance of God's smiles
When we have soared above life's trials.
So when you're overwhelmed with fears
And all your hopes are drenched in tears,
Think not that life has been unfair
And given you too much to bear,
For God has chosen you because,
With all your weaknesses and flaws,
He feels that you are worthy of
The greatness of his wondrous love.

Is the Cross You Wear Too Heavy to Bear?

Complainingly I told myself
   this cross was too heavy to wear,
And I wondered discontentedly
   why God gave it to me to bear.
I looked with envy at others
   whose crosses seemed lighter than mine
And wished that I could change my cross
   for one of a lighter design.
Then in a dream I beheld the cross
   I impulsively wanted to wear—
It was fashioned of pearls and diamonds
   and gems that are precious and rare,

And when I hung it around my neck,
  the weight of the jewels and the gold
Was much too heavy and cumbersome
  for my small, slender neck to hold.
So I tossed it aside, and before my eyes
  was a cross of rose-red flowers,
And I said with delight as I put it on,
  "This cross I can wear for hours."
For it was so dainty and fragile,
  so lovely and light and thin,
But I had forgotten about the thorns
  that started to pierce my skin.
Then in a dream I saw my cross—
  rugged and old and plain—
The clumsy old cross I had looked upon
  with discontented disdain,
And at last I knew that God had made
  this special cross for me,
For God in His great wisdom
  knew what I before could not see—
That often the loveliest crosses
  are the heaviest crosses to bear,
For only God is wise enough
  to choose the cross each can wear.
So never complain about your cross,
  for your cross has been blessed—
God made it just for you to wear
  and remember, God knows best.

Showers of Blessings

Each day there are showers of blessings
    sent from the Father above,
For God is a great, lavish giver,
    and there is no end to His love . . .
And His grace is more than sufficient,
    His mercy is boundless and deep,
And His infinite blessings are countless—
    and all this we're given to keep
If we but seek God and find Him
    And ask for a bounteous measure
Of this wholly immeasurable offering
    from God's inexhaustible treasure . . .
For no matter how big man's dreams are,
    God's blessings are infinitely more,
For always God's giving is greater
    than what man is asking for.

God Is No Stranger

God is no stranger in a faraway place—
He's as close as the wind that blows 'cross my face.
It's true I can't see the wind as it blows,
But I feel it around me and my heart surely knows
That God's mighty hand can be felt everywhere,
For there's nothing on earth that is not in God's care.
The sky and the stars, the waves and the sea,
The dew on the grass, the leaves on a tree
Are constant reminders of God and His nearness,
Proclaiming His presence with crystal-like clearness.
So how could I think God was far, far away
When I feel Him beside me every hour of the day?
And I've plenty of reasons to know God's my Friend,
And this is one friendship that time cannot end.

Blessings Devised by God

God speaks to us in many ways,
Altering our lives, our plans and days,
And His blessings come in many guises
That He alone in love devises,
And sorrow, which we dread so much,
Can bring a very healing touch . . .
For when we fail to heed His voice
We leave the Lord no other choice
Except to use a firm, stern hand
To make us know He's in command . . .
For on the wings of loss and pain,
The peace we often sought in vain
Will come to us with sweet surprise,
For God is merciful and wise . . .
And through dark hours of tribulation
God gives us time for meditation,
And nothing can be counted loss
Which teaches us to bear our cross.

Man Cannot Live by Bread Alone

He lived in a palace on a mountain of gold,
Surrounded by riches and wealth untold,
Priceless possessions and treasures of art,
But he died alone of a hungry heart
For man cannot live by bread alone
No matter what he may have or own,
For though he reaches his earthly goal,
He'll waste away with a starving soul
But he who eats of the holy bread
Will always find his spirit fed,
And even the poorest of men can afford
To feast at the table prepared by the Lord.

God's Love

God's love is like an island
    in life's ocean vast and wide—
A peaceful, quiet shelter
    from the restless, rising tide.
God's love is like an anchor
    when the angry billows roll—
A mooring in the storms of life,
    a stronghold for the soul.
God's love is like a fortress,
    and we seek protection there
When the waves of tribulation
    seem to drown us in despair.
God's love is like a harbor
    where our souls can find sweet rest
From the struggle and the tension
    of life's fast and futile quest.
God's love is like a beacon
    burning bright with faith and prayer,
And, through the changing scenes of life,
    we can find a haven there.

"Love Divine, All Loves Excelling"

In a myriad of miraculous ways
God shapes our lives and changes our days.
Beyond our will or even knowing
God keeps our spirits ever growing . . .
For lights and shadows, sun and rain,
Sadness and gladness, joy and pain
Combine to make our lives complete
And give us victory through defeat.
Oh "Love divine, all loves excelling,"
In troubled hearts You just keep dwelling,
Patiently waiting for a prodigal son
To say at last, "Thy will be done."

Not by Chance or Happenstance

Into our lives come many things
    to break the dull routine—
The things we had not planned on
    that happen unforeseen—
The unexpected little joys
    that are scattered on our way,
Success we did not count on
    or a rare, fulfilling day,
A catchy, lilting melody
    that makes us want to dance,
A nameless exaltation
    of enchantment and romance,
An unsought word of kindness,
    a compliment or two
That set the eyes to gleaming
    like crystal drops of dew,
The sudden, unplanned meeting
    that comes with sweet surprise
And lights the heart with happiness
    like a rainbow in the skies.
Now some folks call it fickle fate
    and some folks call it chance
While others just accept it
    as a pleasant happenstance,
But no matter what you call it,
    it didn't come without design,
For all our lives are fashioned
    by the hand that is divine
And every lucky happening
    and every lucky break
Are little gifts from God above
    that are ours to freely take.

The Hand of God Is Everywhere

It's true we have never looked on His face,
But His likeness shines forth from every place,
For the hand of God is everywhere
Along life's busy thoroughfare,
And His presence can be felt and seen
Right in the midst of our daily routine.
Things we touch and see and feel
Are what make God so very real.

My God Is No Stranger

I've never seen God, but I know how I feel—
It's people like you who make Him so real.
My God is no stranger—He's so friendly each day,
And He doesn't ask me to weep when I pray.
It seems that I pass Him so often each day
In the faces of people I meet on my way.
He's the stars in the heavens, a smile on some face,
A leaf on a tree or a rose in a vase.
He's winter and autumn and summer and spring—
In short, God is every real, wonderful thing.
I wish I might meet Him much more than I do—
I would if there were more people like you.

Spiritual Strength

Life can't always be a song—
You have to have trouble
    to make you strong,
So whenever you are troubled
    and everything goes wrong,
It is just God working in you
    to make your spirit strong.

A Pattern for Living

"Love one another as I have loved you"
May seem impossible to do,
But if you will try to trust and believe,
Great are the joys that you will receive,
For love makes us patient, understanding, and kind,
And we judge with our hearts and not with our minds,
For as soon as love entered the heart's open door,
The faults we once saw are not there any more—
And the things that seemed wrong begin to look right
When viewed in the softness of love's gentle light
For love works in ways that are wondrous and strange,
And there is nothing in life that love cannot change,
And all that God promised will someday come true
When you have loved one another the way He loved you.

A Rainbow of Hope

The rainbow is God's promise
    of hope for you and me,
And though the clouds hang heavy
    and the sun we cannot see,
We know above the dark clouds
    that fill the stormy sky
Hope's rainbow will come shining through
    when the clouds have drifted by.

Beyond Our Asking

More than hearts can imagine
    or minds comprehend,
God's bountiful gifts
    are ours without end.
We ask for a cupful
    when the vast sea is ours,
We pick a small rosebud
    from a garden of flowers,
We reach for a sunbeam
    but the sun still abides,
We draw one short breath
    but there's air on all sides
Whatever we ask for
    falls short of God's giving,
For His greatness exceeds
    every facet of living
And always God's ready
    and eager and willing
To pour out His mercy,
    completely fulfilling
All of man's needs
    for peace, joy, and rest,
For God gives His children
    whatever is best.
Just give Him a chance
    to open His treasures,
And He'll fill your life
    with unfathomable pleasures—
Pleasures that never
    grow worn out and faded
And leave us depleted,
    disillusioned and jaded—
For God has a storehouse
    just filled to the brim
With all that man needs,
    if we'll only ask Him.

Unaware We Pass Him By

On life's busy thoroughfares
We meet with angels unawares,
But we are too busy to listen or hear,
Too busy to sense that God is near,
Too busy to stop and recognize
The grief that lies in another's eyes,
Too busy to offer to help or share,
Too busy to sympathize or care,
Too busy to do the good things we should,
Telling ourselves we would if we could . . .
But life is too swift and the pace is too great,
And we dare not pause, for we might be too late
For our next appointment, which means so much
We are willing to brush off the Savior's touch.
And we tell ourselves there will come a day
When we'll have more time to pause on our way,
But before we know it, life's sun has set,
And we've passed the Savior but never met.
For hurrying along life's thoroughfare,
We passed Him by but remained unaware
That within the very sight of our eyes,
Unnoticed, the Son of God passed by.

Gifts from God

This brings you a million good wishes and more
For the things you cannot buy in a store—
Like faith to sustain you in times of trial,
A joy-filled heart and a happy smile,
Contentment, inner peace, and love—
All priceless gifts from God above!

Somebody Cares

Somebody cares and always will—
The world forgets, but God loves you still.
You cannot go beyond His love
No matter what you're guilty of,
For God forgives until the end—
He is your faithful, loyal Friend . . .
And though you try to hide your face,
There is no shelter any place
That can escape His watchful eye,
For on the earth and in the sky
He's ever-present and always there
To take you in His tender care
And bind the wounds and mend the breaks
When all the world around forsakes.
Somebody cares and loves you still,
And God is the Someone who always will.

God Loves Us

We are all God's children
    and He loves us, every one.
He freely and completely
    forgives all that we have done,
Asking only if we're ready
    to follow where He leads,
Content that in His wisdom
    He will answer all our needs.

God's Jewels for You

We watch the rich and famous
    bedecked in precious jewels,
Enjoying earthly pleasures,
    defying moral rules,
And in our mood of discontent
    we sink into despair
And long for earthly riches
    and feel cheated of our share . . .
But stop these idle musings—
    God has stored up for you
Treasures that are far beyond
    earth's jewels and riches, too,
For never, never discount
    what God has promised man
If he will walk in meekness
    and accept God's flawless plan,
For if we heed His teachings
    as we journey through the years,
We'll find the richest jewels of all
    are crystallized from tears.

God's Waiting to Share

When you're troubled and worried and sick at heart
And your plans are upset and your world falls apart,
Remember God's ready and waiting to share
The burden you find too heavy to bear . . .
So with faith, let go and let God lead the way
Into a brighter and less-troubled day.
For God has a plan for everyone,
If we learn to pray, "Thy will be done."
For nothing in life is without God's design
For each life is fashioned by the hand that's divine.

Seek First the Kingdom of God

Life is a mixture of sunshine and rain,
Good things and bad things, pleasure and pain.
We can't have all sunshine, but it's certainly true
That there's never a cloud the sun doesn't shine through . . .
So always remember, whatever betide you,
The power of God is always beside you . . .
And if friends disappoint you and plans go astray
And nothing works out in just the right way,
And you feel you have failed in achieving your goal
And that life wrongly placed you in an unfitting role,
Take heart and stand tall and think who you are,
For God is your Father and no one can bar
Or keep you from reaching your desired success
Or withhold the joy that is yours to possess . . .
For with God on your side, it matters not who
Is working to keep life's good things from you,
For you need nothing more than God's guidance and love
To insure you the things that you're most worthy of . . .
So trust in His wisdom and follow His ways
And be not concerned with the world's empty praise,
But first seek His kingdom and you will possess
The world's greatest of riches, which is true happiness.

Somebody Loves You

Somebody loves you more than you know,
Somebody goes with you wherever you go,
Somebody really and truly cares
And lovingly listens to all of your prayers . . .
Don't doubt for a minute that this is not true,
For God loves His children and takes care of them, too . . .
And all of His treasures are yours to share
If you love Him completely and show that you care . . .
And if you walk in His footsteps and have faith to believe,
There's nothing you ask for that you will not receive!

God Is the Answer

We read the headlines daily and we listen to the news;
We are anxious and bewildered with the world's conflicting views.
We are restless and dissatisfied and sadly insecure,
And we voice our discontentment over things we must endure.
For this violent age we live in is filled with nameless fears
That grow as we discuss things that come daily to our ears.
So instead of reading headlines that disturb the heart and mind,
Let us open up the Bible, for in doing so we'll find
That this age is no different from the millions gone before
And in every hour of crisis God has opened up a door
For all who sought His guidance and trusted in His plan,
For God provides the answer that cannot be found by man.
And though there's hate and violence and dissension all around,
We can always find a refuge that is built on solid ground.
If we go to God believing in the things we cannot see,
Then can all nations be united in the peace that makes men free . . .
So as we pray for guidance, may a troubled world revive
Faith in God and confidence so our nation may survive,
And draw us ever closer to God and to each other
Until every stranger is a friend and every man a brother.

Memories

Tender little memories
Of some word or deed
Give us strength and courage
When we are in need.
Blessed little memories
Help us bear the cross
And soften all the bitterness
Of failure and loss.
Precious little memories
Of little things we've done
Make the very darkest day
A bright and happy one.

God Will Not Fail You

When life seems empty
　　and there's no place to go,
When your heart is troubled
　　and your spirits are low,
When friends seem few
　　and nobody cares—
There is always God
　　to hear your prayers . . .
And whatever you're facing
　　will seem much less
When you go to God
　　and confide and confess,
For the burden that seems
　　too heavy to bear
God lifts away
　　on the wings of prayer . . .
And seen through God's eyes
　　earthly troubles diminish
And we're given new strength
　　to face and to finish
Life's daily tasks
　　as they come along
If we pray for strength
　　to keep us strong . . .
So go to our Father
　　when troubles assail you,
For His grace is sufficient
　　and He'll never fail you.

What More Can You Ask?

God's love endureth forever—
    what a wonderful thing to know
When the tides of life run against you
    and your spirit is downcast and low.
God's kindness is ever around you
    always ready to freely impart
Strength to your faltering spirit,
    cheer to your lonely heart.
God's presence is ever beside you,
    as near as the reach of your hand.
You have but to tell Him your troubles—
    there is nothing He won't understand . . .
And knowing God's love is unfailing,
    and His mercy unending and great,
You have but to trust in His promise—
    "God comes not too soon or too late" . . .
So wait with a heart that is patient
    for the goodness of God to prevail,
For never do prayers go unanswered,
    and His mercy and love never fail.

Enfolded in His Love

The love of God surrounds us
Like the air we breathe around us—
As near as a heartbeat,
    as close as a prayer,
And whenever we need Him,
    He'll always be there!

God's Assurance Gives Us Endurance

My blessings are so many,
    my troubles are so few—
How can I be discouraged
    when I know that I have You?
And I have the sweet assurance
    that there's nothing I need fear
If I but keep remembering
    I am Yours and You are near,
Help me to endure the storms
    that keep raging deep inside me,
And make me more aware each day
    that no evil can betide me.
If I remain undaunted
    though the billows sweep and roll,
Knowing I have Your assurance,
    there's a haven for my soul,
For anything and everything
    can somehow be endured
If Your presence is beside me
    and lovingly assured.

Why Am I Complaining?

My cross is not too heavy,
    my road is not too rough
Because God walks beside me,
    and to know this is enough . . .
And though I get so lonely,
    I know I'm not alone,
For the Lord God is my Father
    and He loves me as His own . . .
So though I'm tired and weary
    and I wish my race were run,

God will only terminate it
    when my work on earth is done . . .
So let me stop complaining
    about my load of care,
For God will always lighten it
    when it gets too much to bear . . .
And if He does not ease my load,
    He'll give me strength to bear it,
For God, in love and mercy,
    is always near to share it.

He Loves You

It's amazing and incredible,
    but it's as true as it can be—
God loves and understands us all,
    and that means you and me.
His grace is all-sufficient
    for both the young and old,
For the lonely and the timid,
    for the brash and for the bold.
His love knows no exceptions,
    so never feel excluded—
No matter who or what you are,
    your name has been included . . .
And no matter what your past has been,
    trust God to understand,
And no matter what your problem is,
    just place it in His hand . . .
For in all of our unloveliness
    this great God loves us still—
He loved us since the world began,
    and, what's more, He always will!

In God Is Our Strength

It's a troubled world we live in,
    and we wish that we might find
Not only happiness of heart
    but longed-for peace of mind . . .
But where can we begin our search
    in the age of automation,
With neighbor against neighbor
    and nation against nation,
Where values have no permanence
    and change is all around,
And everything is sinking sand
    and nothing solid ground?
Have we placed our faith in leaders
    unworthy of our trust?
Have we lost our own identities
    and allowed our souls to rust?
Have we forgotten Babylon
    and Egypt, Rome, and Greece,
And all the mighty rulers
    who lived by war, not peace,
Who built their thrones and empires
    on power and manmade things
And never knew God's greatness
    or that He is King of kings?
But we've God's Easter promise,
    so let us seek a goal
That opens up new vistas
    for man's eternal soul . . .
For our strength and our security
    lie not in earthly things
But in Christ the Lord, who died for us
    and rose as King of kings.

"In Him We Live, and Move, and Have Our Being"

We walk in a world that is strange and unknown,
And in the midst of the crowd we still feel alone.
We question our purpose, our part, and our place
In this vast land of mystery suspended in space.
We probe and explore and try hard to explain
The tumult of thoughts that our minds entertain,
But all of our problems and complex explanations
Of man's inner feelings and fears and frustrations
Still leave us engulfed in the mystery of life
With all of its struggles and suffering and strife,
Unable to fathom what tomorrow will bring—
But there is one truth to which we can cling . . .
For while life's a mystery man can't understand,
The great Giver of life is holding our hands,
And safe in His care there is no need for seeing,
"For in Him we live, and move, and have our being."

God Bless and Keep You in His Care

There are many things in life
    we cannot understand,
But we must trust God's judgment
    and be guided by His hand . . .
And all who have God's blessing
    can rest safely in His care,
For He promises safe passage
    on the wings of faith and prayer.

God Is Never beyond Our Reach

No one ever sought the Father
   and found He was not there,
And no burden is too heavy
   to be lightened by a prayer.
No problem is too intricate,
   and no sorrow that we face
Is too deep and devastating
   to be softened by His grace.
No trials and tribulations
   are beyond what we can bear
If we share them with our Father
   as we talk to Him in prayer . . .
And men of every color,
   every race, and every creed
Have but to seek the Father
   in their deepest hour of need.
God asks for no credentials—
   He accepts us with our flaws.
He is kind and understanding
   and He welcomes us because
We are His erring children
   and He loves us, every one,
And He freely and completely
   forgives all that we have done,
Asking only if we're ready
   to follow where He leads,
Content that in His wisdom
   He will answer all our needs.

About Prayer
and Prayers

Inspiration! Meditation! Dedication!

Brighten your day
And lighten your way
And lessen your cares
With daily prayers.
Quiet your mind
And leave tension behind
And find inspiration
In hushed meditation.

The Mystery of Prayer

Beyond that which words can interpret
    or theology explain,
The soul feels a shower of refreshment
    that falls like the gentle rain
On hearts that are parched with problems
    and are searching to find the way
To somehow attract God's attention
    through well-chosen words as they pray,
Not knowing that God in His wisdom
    can sense all man's worry and woe,
For there is nothing man can conceal
    that God does not already know . . .
So kneel in prayer in His presence
    and you'll find no need to speak,
For softly in quiet communion,
    God grants you the peace that you seek.

Not What You Want, but What God Wills

Do you want what you want when you want it,
    do you pray and expect a reply?
And when it's not instantly answered,
    do you feel that God passed you by?
Well, prayers that are prayed in this manner
    are really not prayers at all,
For you can't go to God in a hurry
    and expect Him to answer your call.
For prayers are not meant for obtaining
    what we selfishly wish to acquire,
For God in His wisdom refuses
    the things that we wrongly desire . . .
And don't pray for freedom from trouble
    or pray that life's trials pass you by.
Instead pray for strength and for courage
    to meet life's dark hours and not cry
That God was not there when you called Him
    and He turned a deaf ear to your prayer
And just when you needed Him most of all
    He left you alone in despair.
Wake up! You are missing completely
    the reason and purpose of prayer,
Which is really to keep us contented
    that God holds us safe in His care . . .
And God only answers our pleadings
    when He knows that our wants fill a need,
And whenever our will becomes His will
    There is no prayer that God does not heed.

The Soul of Man

Every man has a deep heart need
That cannot be filled with doctrine or creed,
For the soul of man knows nothing more
Than just that he is longing for
A haven that is safe and sure,
A fortress where he feels secure,
An island in this sea of strife,
Away from all the storms of life.
Oh, God of love, who sees us all,
You are so great—we are so small.
Hear man's universal prayer
Crying to You in despair—
"Save my soul and grant me peace,
Let my restless murmurings cease.
God of love, forgive—forgive.
Teach me how to truly live.
Ask me not my race or creed,
Just take me in my hour of need
And let me know You love me, too,
And that I am a part of You"
And someday may man realize
That all the earth, the seas, and skies
Belong to God, who made us all—
The rich, the poor, the great, the small—
And in the Father's holy sight
No man is yellow, black, or white . . .
And peace on earth cannot be found
Until we meet on common ground
And every man becomes a brother
Who worships God and loves each other.

"Thy Will Be Done"

God did not promise
    sun without rain,
Light without darkness
    or joy without pain.
He only promised
    strength for the day
When the darkness comes
    and we lose our way . . .
For only through sorrow
    do we grow more aware
That God is our refuge
    in times of despair,
For when we are happy
    and life's bright and fair,
We often forget
    to kneel down in prayer . . .
But God seems much closer
    and needed much more
When trouble and sorrow
    stand outside our door,
For then we seek shelter
    in His wondrous love,
And we ask Him to send us
    help from above . . .
And that is the reason
    we know it is true
That bright, shining hours
    and dark, sad ones, too,
Are part of the plan
    God made for each one,
And all we can pray
    is "Thy will be done."
And know that you
    are never alone,
For God is your Father
    and you're one of His own.

Anywhere Is a Place of Prayer If God Is There

I have prayed on my knees in the morning,
  I have prayed as I walked along,
I have prayed in the silence and darkness,
  and I've prayed to the tune of a song.
I have prayed in the midst of a triumph,
  and I've prayed when I suffered defeat—
I have prayed on the sands of the seashore
  where the waves of the ocean beat.
I have prayed in a velvet, hushed forest
  where the quietness calmed my fears—
I have prayed through suffering and heartache
  when my eyes were blinded with tears.
I have prayed in churches and chapels,
  cathedrals and synagogues, too,
But often I had the feeling
  that my prayers were not getting through . . .
And I realized then that our Father
  is not really concerned where we pray
Or impressed by our manner of worship
  or the eloquent words that we say.
He is only concerned with our feelings,
  and He looks deep into our hearts
And hears the cry of our souls' deep need
  that no words could ever impart . . .
So it isn't the prayer that's expressive
  or offered in some special spot—
It's the sincere plea of a sinner,
  and God can tell whether or not
We honestly seek His forgiveness
  and earnestly mean what we say,
And then and then only God answers
  the prayers that we fervently pray.

Breakfast for the Soul

I meet God in the morning
    and go with Him through the day,
Then in the stillness of the night
    before sleep comes I pray
That God will just take over
    all the problems I couldn't solve,
And in the peacefulness of sleep
    my cares will all dissolve.
So when I open up my eyes
    to greet another day,
I'll find myself renewed in strength
    and there will open up a way
To meet what seemed impossible
    for me to solve alone,
And once again I'll be assured
    I am never on my own.

A Special Prayer for You

I said a special prayer for you—
    I asked the Lord above
To keep you safely in His care
    and enfold you in His love.
I did not ask for fortune,
    for riches or for fame,
I only asked for blessings
    in the Holy Savior's name—
Blessings to surround you
    in times of trial and stress,
And inner joy to fill your heart
    with peace and happiness.

What Is Prayer?

Is it measured words that are memorized,
Forcefully said and dramatized,
Offered with pomp and with arrogant pride
In words unmatched to the feelings inside?
No, prayer is so often just words unspoken,
Whispered in tears by a heart that is broken,
For God is already deeply aware
Of the burdens we find too heavy to bear . . .
And all we need do is seek Him in prayer
And without a word He will help us to bear
Our trials and troubles, our sickness and sorrow
And show us the way to a brighter tomorrow.
There's no need at all for impressive prayer,
For the minute we seek God He's already there.

The House of Prayer

Just close your eyes and open your heart
And feel your cares and worries depart.
Just yield yourself to the Father above
And let Him hold you secure in His love . . .
For life on earth grows more involved
With endless problems that can't be solved,
But God only asks us to do our best—
Then He will take over and finish the rest . . .
So when you are tired, discouraged, and blue,
There's always one door that is opened to you
And that is the door to the house of prayer,
And you'll find God waiting to meet you there . . .
And the house of prayer is no farther away
Than the quiet spot where you kneel and pray,

For the heart is a temple when God is there
As we place ourselves in His loving care . . .
And He hears every prayer and answers each one
When we pray in His name, "Thy will be done."
And the burdens that seemed too heavy to bear
Are lifted away on the wings of prayer.

God Is Always There to Hear Our Prayer

Let us find joy
    in the news of His birth,
And let us find comfort
    and strength for each day
In knowing that Christ
    walked this same earthly way,
So He knows all our needs
    and He hears every prayer,
And He keeps all His children
    always safe in His care . . .
And whenever we're troubled
    and lost in despair,
We have but to seek Him
    and ask Him in prayer
To guide and direct us
    and help us to bear
Our sickness and sorrow,
    our worry and care . . .
So once more at Christmas
    let the whole world rejoice
In the knowledge He answers
    every prayer that we voice.

Prayers Can't Be Answered until They Are Prayed

Life without purpose
  is barren indeed—
There can't be a harvest
  unless you plant seed.
There can't be attainment
  unless there's a goal,
And man's but a robot
  unless there's a soul.
If we send no ships out,
  no ships will come in,
And unless there's a contest,
  nobody can win . . .
For games can't be won
  unless they are played,
And prayers can't be answered
  unless they are prayed . . .
So whatever is wrong
  with your life today,
You'll find a solution
  if you kneel down and pray
Not just for pleasure,
  enjoyment, and health,
Not just for honors,
  prestige, and wealth,
But pray for a purpose
  to make life worth living,
And pray for the joy
  of unselfish giving . . .
For great is your gladness
  and rich your reward
When you make your life's purpose
  the choice of the Lord.

I Think of You and I Pray for You Too

Often during a busy day
I pause for a minute to silently pray,
I mention the names of those I love
And treasured friends I am fondest of—
For it doesn't matter where we pray
If we honestly mean the words that we say,
For God is always listening to hear
The prayers that are made by a heart that's sincere.

No Prayer Goes Unheard

Often we pause and wonder
   when we kneel down and pray
Can God really hear
   the prayers that we say?
But if we keep praying
   and talking to Him,
He'll brighten the soul
   that was clouded and dim
And as we continue,
   our burden seems lighter,
Our sorrow is softened
   and our outlook is brighter.
For though we feel helpless
   and alone when we start,
A prayer is the key
   that opens the heart,
And as the heart opens,
   the dear Lord comes in
And the prayer that we felt
   we could never begin
Is so easy to say,
   for the Lord understands
And He gives us new strength
   by the touch of His hands.

On the Wings of Prayer

On the wings of prayer
   our burdens take flight
And our load of care
   becomes bearably light
And our heavy hearts
   are lifted above
To be healed by the balm
   of God's wonderful love . . .
And the tears in our eyes
   are dried by the hands
Of a loving Father
   who understands
All of our problems,
   our fears and despair
When we take them to Him
   on the wings of prayer.

The Heavenly Staircase

Prayers are the stairs that lead to God,
   and there's joy every step of the way
When we make our pilgrimage to Him
   with love in our hearts each day.

A Prayer That God Will Keep You in His Care

Prayers for big and little things
Fly heavenward on angels' wings . . .
And He who walked by the Galilee
And touched the blind and made them see
And cured the man who long was lame
When he but called God's holy name
Will keep you safely in His care,
And when you need Him, He'll be there.

Let Your Wish Become a Prayer

Put your dearest wish in God's hands today
And discuss it with Him as you faithfully pray,
And you can be sure your wish will come true
If God feels your wish will be good for you . . .
There's no problem too big and no question too small—
Just ask God in faith and He'll answer them all—
Not always at once, so be patient and wait,
For God never comes too soon or too late . . .
So trust in His wisdom and believe in His word,
For no prayer's unanswered and no prayer's unheard.

Daily Prayers Are Heaven's Stars

The stairway rises heaven-high,
    the steps are dark and steep.
In weariness we climb them
    as we stumble, fall, and weep . . .
And many times we falter
    along the path of prayer,
Wondering if You hear us
    and if You really care.
Oh, give us some assurance,
    restore our faith anew,
So we can keep on climbing
    the stairs of prayer to You . . .
For we are weak and wavering,
    uncertain and unsure,
And only meeting You in prayer
    can help us to endure
All life's trials and troubles,
    its sickness, pain, and sorrow
And give us strength and courage
    to face and meet tomorrow.

Begin Each Day by Kneeling to Pray

Start every day
    with a "good morning" prayer
And God will bless each thing you do
    and keep you in His care . . .
And never, never sever
    the spirit's silken strand
That our Father up in heaven
    holds in His mighty hand.

Daily Prayers Dissolve Your Cares

We all have cares and problems
    we cannot solve alone,
But if we go to God in prayer,
    we are never on our own,
And if we try to stand alone,
    we are weak and we will fall,
For God is always greatest
    when we're helpless, lost, and small . . .
And no day is unmeetable
    if, on rising, our first thought
Is to thank God for the blessings
    that His loving care has brought,
For there can be no failures
    or hopeless, unsaved sinners
If we enlist the help of God,
    who makes all losers winners . . .
So meet Him in the morning
    and go with Him through the day
And thank Him for His guidance
    each evening when you pray—

And if you follow faithfully
   this daily way to pray,
You will never in your lifetime
   face another hopeless day . . .
For, like a soaring eagle,
   you too can rise above
The storms of life around you
   on the wings of prayer and love.

Let Not Your Heart Be Troubled

Whenever I am troubled
   and lost in deep despair,
I bundle all my troubles up
   and go to God in prayer . . .
I tell Him I am heartsick
   and lost and lonely, too,
That my mind is deeply burdened
   and I don't know what to do . . .
But I know He stilled the tempest
   and calmed the angry sea,
And I humbly ask if, in His love,
   He'll do the same for me . . .
And then I just keep quiet
   and think only thoughts of peace,
And if I abide in stillness
   my restless murmurings cease.

Heart Song

There are so many, many times
    God seems so far away
That I can't help but wonder
    if He hears me when I pray.
Then I beseech Him earnestly
    to hear my humble plea
And tell me how to serve Him
    and to do it gallantly . . .
And so I pray this little prayer
    and hope that He will show me
How I can bring more happiness
    to all the folks who know me—
And give me hope and courage,
    enough for every day,
And faith to light the darkness
    when I stumble on my way,
And love and understanding,
    enough to make me kind,
So I may judge all people
    with my heart and not my mind.

The First Thing Every Morning, and the Last Thing Every Night

Were you too busy this morning
    to quietly stop and pray?
Did you hurry and drink your coffee
    then frantically rush away,
Consoling yourself by saying—
    God will always be there
Waiting to hear my petitions,
    ready to answer each prayer?

It's true that the great, generous Savior
    forgives our transgressions each day
And patiently waits for lost sheep
    who constantly seem to stray,
But moments of prayer once omitted
    in the busy rush of the day
Can never again be recaptured,
    for they silently slip away.
Strength is gained in the morning
    to endure the trials of the day
When we visit with God in person
    in a quiet and unhurried way,
For only through prayer that's unhurried
    can the needs of the day be met
And only in prayers said at evening
    can we sleep without fears or regret.
For all of our errors and failures
    that we made in the course of the day
Are freely forgiven at nighttime
    when we kneel down and earnestly pray,
So seek the Lord in the morning
    and never forget Him at night,
For prayer is an unfailing blessing
    that makes every burden seem light.

Talk It Over with God

You're worried and troubled
    about everything,
Wondering and fearing
    what tomorrow will bring.
You long to tell someone,
    for you feel so alone,
But your friends are all burdened
    with cares of their own.
There is only one place
    and only one Friend
Who is never too busy,
    and you can always depend
On Him to be waiting,
    with arms open wide,
To hear all the troubles
    you came to confide . . .
For the heavenly Father
    will always be there
When you seek Him and find Him
    at the altar of prayer.

Renewal

When life has lost its luster
    and it's filled with dull routine,
When you long to run away from it,
    seeking pastures new and green,
Remember, no one runs away from life
    without finding when they do
That you can't escape the thoughts you think
    that are pressing down on you—
For though the scenery may be different,
    it's the same old heart and mind
And the same old restless longings
    that you tried to leave behind . . .

So when your heart is heavy
   and your day is dull with care,
Instead of trying to escape,
   why not withdraw in prayer?
For in prayer there is renewal
   of the spirit, mind, and heart,
For everything is lifted up
   in which God has a part—
For when we go to God in prayer,
   our thoughts are rearranged,
So even though our problems
   have not been solved or changed,
Somehow the good Lord gives us
   the power to understand
That He who holds tomorrow
   is the One who holds our hands.

My Prayer

Bless me, heavenly Father,
   forgive my erring ways.
Grant me strength to serve Thee,
   put purpose in my days.
Give me understanding,
   enough to make me kind
So I may judge all people
   with my heart and not my mind.
Teach me to be patient
   in everything I do,
Content to trust your wisdom
   and to follow after You.
Help me when I falter
   and hear me when I pray,
And receive me in Thy kingdom
   to dwell with Thee someday.

Not to Seek, Lord, but to Share

Dear God, much too often
   we seek You in prayer
Because we are wallowing
   in our own self-despair.
We make every word
   we lamentingly speak
An imperative plea
   for whatever we seek.
We pray for ourselves
   and so seldom for others—
We're concerned with our problems
   and not with our brothers.
We seem to forget, Lord,
   that the sweet hour of prayer
Is not for self-seeking
   but to place in Your care
All the lost souls,
   unloved and unknown,
And to keep praying for them
   until they're Your own.
For it's never enough
   to seek God in prayer
With no thought of others
   who are lost in despair.
So teach us, dear God,
   that the power of prayer
Is made stronger by placing
   the world in Your care.

A Part of Me

Dear God, You are a part of me—
You're all I do and all I see,
You're what I say and what I do,
For all my life belongs to You.

You walk with me and talk with me,
For I am Yours eternally,
And when I stumble, slip, and fall
Because I'm weak and lost and small,
You help me up and take my hand
And lead me toward the Promised Land.
I cannot dwell apart from You—
You would not ask or want me to,
For You have room within Your heart
To make each child of Yours a part
Of You and all Your love and care
If we but come to You in prayer.

I Meet God in the Morning

Each day at dawning
   I lift my heart high
And raise up my eyes
   to the infinite sky.
I watch the night vanish
   as a new day is born,
And I hear the birds sing
   on the wings of the morn.
I see the dew glisten
   in crystal-like splendor
While God, with a touch
   that is gentle and tender,
Wraps up the night
   and softly tucks it away
And hangs out the sun
   to herald a new day . . .
And so I give thanks
   and my heart kneels to pray,
"God, keep me and guide me
   and go with me today."

Good Morning, God

You are ushering in another day,
    untouched and freshly new,
So here I am to ask You, God,
    if You'll renew me, too . . .
Forgive the many errors
    that I made yesterday
And let me try again, dear God,
    to walk closer in Thy way . . .
But, Father, I am well aware
    I can't make it on my own,
So take my hand and hold it tight,
    for I can't walk alone.

My Daily Prayer

God, be my resting place
    and my protection
In hours of trouble,
    defeat, and dejection—
May I never give way
    to self-pity and sorrow,
May I always be sure
    of a better tomorrow,
May I stand undaunted,
    come what may,
Secure in the knowledge
    I have only to pray
And ask my Creator
    and Father above
To keep me serene
    in His grace and His love.

Help Us to See and Understand

God, give us wider vision
   to see and understand
That both the sunshine and the showers
   are gifts from Thy great hand,
And when our lives are overcast
   with trouble and with care,
Give us faith to see beyond
   the dark clouds of despair,
And give us strength to rise above
   the mist of doubt and fear,
And recognize the hidden smile
   behind each burning tear . . .
And teach us that it takes the showers
   to make the flowers grow,
And only in the storms of life
   when the winds of trouble blow
Can man too reach maturity
   and grow in faith and grace
And gain the strength and courage
   to enable him to face
Sunny days as well as rain,
   high peaks as well as low,
Knowing that the April showers
   will make May flowers grow . . .
And then at last may we accept
   the sunshine and the showers,
Confident it takes them both
   to make salvation ours.

Show Me the Way to Serve and Love You More

God, help me in my feeble way
To somehow do something each day
To show You that I love You best
And that my faith will stand each test,
And let me serve You every day
And feel You near me when I pray.
Oh, hear my prayer, dear God above,
And make me worthy of Your love.

A Child's Prayer

Hear me, blessed Jesus,
    as I say my prayers today
And tell me You are close to me
    and You'll never go away . . .
And tell me that You love me
    like the Bible says You do,
And tell me also, Jesus,
    I can always come to You
And You will understand me
    when other people don't,
And though some may forget me,
    just tell me that You won't . . .
And, Jesus, stay real close to me
    at home and school and play,
For I will feel much braver
    if You're never far away . . .
And sometimes when I'm naughty,
    I hope You won't be sad,
For really I don't mean to do
    anything that's bad . . .
And most of all, dear Jesus,
    it's Your birthday, and I know

Your Father sent You to us
 to live on earth below
So little children like myself
 would know You too were small
And that You are our dearest Friend
 and that You understand us all . . .
And, Jesus, I like Christmas
 and the presents that it brings,
But I know Your love is greater
 than all the other things . . .
And some day when I'm older,
 I will show You it is true
That even as a little child
 my heart belongs to You.

Widen My Vision

God, open my eyes so I may see
And feel Your presence close to me.
Give me strength for my stumbling feet
As I battle the crowd on life's busy street,
And widen the vision of my unseeing eyes
So in passing faces I'll recognize
Not just a stranger, unloved and unknown,
But a friend with a heart that is much like my own.
Give me perception to make me aware
That scattered profusely on life's thoroughfare
Are the best gifts of God that we daily pass by
As we look at the world with an unseeing eye.

No Favor Do I Seek Today

I come not to ask, to plead, or implore You—
I just come to tell You how much I adore You.
For to kneel in Your presence makes me feel blessed,
For I know that You know all my needs best,
And it fills me with joy just to linger with You,
As my soul You replenish and my heart You renew.
For prayer is much more than just asking for things—
It's the peace and contentment that quietness brings.
So thank You again for Your mercy and love
And for making me heir to Your kingdom above.

God, Are You Really Real?

I want to believe, I want to be true,
I want to be loyal and faithful to You,
But where can I go when vague doubts arise
And when evil appears in an angel's disguise
While clamoring voices demand my attention
And the air is polluted with cries of dissension?
You know, God, it's easy just to follow the crowd
Who are doing their thing while shouting out loud
Gross protestations against the old rules
That limit and hamper the new freedom schools.
God, answer this prayer and tell me the truth—
Are You really the God both of age and of youth?
And, God, speak to my heart so I truly feel
That these prophets are false but You really are real.

God, Are You There?

I'm way down here—
    You're way up there.
Are You sure You can hear
    my faint, faltering prayer?
For I'm so unsure
    of just how to pray—
To tell You the truth, God,
    I don't know what to say.
I just know I'm lonely
    and vaguely disturbed,
Bewildered and restless,
    confused and perturbed,
And they tell me that prayer
    helps to quiet the mind
And to unburden the heart,
    for in stillness we find
A newborn assurance
    that Someone does care
And Someone does answer
    each small, sincere prayer.

A Prayer of Thanks

Thank You, God, for the beauty
    around me everywhere,
The gentle rain and glistening dew,
    the sunshine and the air,
The joyous gift of feeling
    the soul's soft, whispering voice
That speaks to me from deep within
    and makes my heart rejoice.

It's Me Again, God

Remember me, God?
 I come every day
Just to talk with You, Lord,
 and to learn how to pray.
You make me feel welcome,
 You reach out Your hand.
I need never explain,
 for You understand.
I come to You frightened
 and burdened with care,
So lonely and lost
 and so filled with despair,
And suddenly, Lord,
 I'm no longer afraid—
My burden is lighter
 and the dark shadows fade.
Oh, God, what a comfort
 to know that You care
And to know when I seek You,
 You will always be there.

More of Thee—Less of Me

Take me and break me and make me, dear God,
 just what You want me to be.
Give me the strength to accept what You send
 and eyes with the vision to see
All the small, arrogant ways that I have
 and the vain little things that I do.
Make me aware that I'm often concerned
 more with myself than with You.
Uncover before me my weakness and greed
 and help me to search deep inside

So I may discover how easy it is
   to be selfishly lost in my pride . . .
And then in Thy goodness and mercy,
   look down on this weak, erring one
And tell me that I am forgiven
   for all I've so willfully done,
And teach me to humbly start following
   the path that the dear Savior trod
So I'll find at the end of life's journey
   a home in the city of God.

He Understands

Although it sometimes seems to us
   our prayers have not been heard,
God always knows our every need
   without a single word,
And He will not forsake us
   even though the way is steep,
For always He is near to us,
   a tender watch to keep . . .
And in good time He will answer us,
   and in His love He'll send
Greater things than we have asked
   and blessings without end . . .
So though we do not understand
   why trouble comes to man,
Can we not be contented
   just to know it is God's plan?

Power of Prayer

I am only a worker employed by the Lord,
And great is my gladness and rich my reward
If I can just spread the wonderful story
That God is the answer to eternal glory . . .
And only the people who read my poems
Can help me to reach more hearts and homes,
Bringing new hope and comfort and cheer
Telling sad hearts there is nothing to fear,
And what greater joy could there be than to share
The love of God and the power of prayer.

I commend you into God's hands, and there is no safer place
In all the universe in which to leave anyone than in the
    hands of God.

Peace, Stillness, and Solitude

A Prayer for Peace and Patience

God, teach me to be patient,
    teach me to go slow—
Teach me how to wait on You
    when my way I do not know.
Teach me sweet forbearance
    when things do not go right
So I remain unruffled
    when others grow uptight.
Teach me how to quiet
    my racing, rising heart
So I might hear the answer
    You are trying to impart.
Teach me to let go, dear God,
    and pray undisturbed until
My heart is filled with inner peace
    and I learn to know Your will.

A Prayer for Peace

Give us strength and courage
    to be honorable and true
And to place our trust implicitly
    in unseen things and You . . .
And keep us kind and humble
    and fill our hearts with love,
Which in this selfish, greedy world
    man has so little of.
Forgive us our transgressions
    and help us find the way
To a better world for everyone
    where man walks in peace each day.

What Does God Know of These Modern Days?

He sent His Son to live on earth
  and to walk with sinful men,
And the problems that confront us
  are the same today as then . . .
For vice and crime and evil
  prevailed in Rome and Greece,
And power-driven demagogues
  incited war not peace.
There was violence and dissension
  and injustice in high courts,
And slayings were accepted
  as one of the favorite sports.
Depraved, debauched, and dissolute,
  men lusted after pleasure—
They knew no god but power,
  and gold was their only treasure . . .
So all the things we face today
  are certainly not new,
And the Son of God experienced
  everything we're going through . . .
So let no one mislead you
  with that hackneyed little phrase
That there's a many-century gap
  between God and modern days . . .
For God has seen a lot of worlds
  in this same tragic state,
And He knows that we're headed for
  the same grim, terrible fate
Unless man is awakened
  before the hour's too late
And at long last realizes
  that God's always up-to-date.

Now I Lay Me Down to Sleep

I remember so well this prayer I said
Each night as my mother tucked me in bed,
And today this same prayer is still the best way
To sign off with God at the end of the day
And to ask Him your soul to safely keep
As you wearily close your tired eyes in sleep,
Feeling content that the Father above
Will hold you secure in His great arms of love . . .
And having His promise that if ere you wake
His angels reach down, your sweet soul to take
Is perfect assurance that, awake or asleep,
God is always right there to tenderly keep
All of His children ever safe in His care,
For God's here and He's there and He's everywhere . . .
So into His hands each night as I sleep
I commend my soul for the dear Lord to keep,
Knowing that if my soul should take flight
It will soar to the land where there is no night.

So Swift the Way! So Short the Day!

In this fast-moving world of turmoil and tension,
With problems and troubles too many to mention,
Our days are so crowded and our hours so few—
There's so little time and so much to do.
We are pressured and pushed until we are dizzy—
There's never a minute we're not crazily busy.
And sometimes we wonder as we rush through the day—
Does God really want us to hurry this way?
Why are we impatient and continually vexed
And often bewildered, disturbed, and perplexed?
Perhaps we're too busy with our own selfish seeking
To hear the dear Lord when He's tenderly speaking.

We are working so tensely in our self-centered way,
We've no time for listening to what God has to say.
And as hard as we work, at the end of the day,
We know in our hearts we did not pay our way,
But God in His mercy looks down on us all,
And though what we've done may be pitifully small,
He makes us feel welcome to kneel down and pray
For the chance to do better as we start a new day.
And life would be better if we learned to rely
On our Father in heaven without asking why
And if we'd remember as we rushed through the day,
The Lord is our Shepherd and He'll lead the way.
So don't rush ahead in reckless endeavor—
Remember He leadeth, and time is forever.

Listen in the Quietness

To try to run away from life
 is impossible to do,
For no matter where you chance to go,
 your troubles will follow you—
For though the scenery is different,
 when you look deep inside you'll find
The same deep, restless longings
 that you thought you left behind . . .
So when life becomes a problem
 much too great for us to bear,
Instead of trying to escape,
 let us withdraw in prayer—
For withdrawal means renewal
 if we withdraw to pray
And listen in the quietness
 to hear what God will say.

The Prayer of Peace

Our Father up in heaven,
  hear this fervent prayer—
May the people of all nations
  be united in Thy care . . .
For earth's peace and man's salvation
  can come only by Thy grace
And not through bombs and missiles
  and our quest for outer space . . .
For until all men recognize
  that the battle is the Lord's
And peace on earth cannot be won
  with strategy and swords,
We will go on vainly fighting
  as we have in ages past,
Finding only empty victories
  and a peace that cannot last . . .
But we've grown so rich and mighty
  and so arrogantly strong
We no longer ask in humbleness—
  God, show us where we're wrong.
We have come to trust completely in
  the power of manmade things,
Unmindful of God's mighty power
  and that He is King of kings.
We have turned our eyes away from Him
  to go our selfish way,
And money, power, and pleasure
  are the gods we serve today . . .
And the good green earth God gave us
  to peacefully enjoy,
Through greed and fear and hatred
  we are seeking to destroy.
Oh Father up in heaven,
  stir and wake our sleeping souls,
Renew our faith and lift us up
  and give us higher goals,

And grant us heavenly guidance
as war threatens us again—
For, more than guided missiles,
all the world needs guided men.

The Fortress of Peace Is Within

Peace is not something you fight for
with bombs and missiles that kill—
Peace is attained in the silence
that comes when the heart stands still . . .
For hearts that are restless and warlike
with longings that never cease
Can never contribute ideas
that bring the world nearer to peace . . .
For as dew never falls on a morning
that follows a dark, stormy night,
The peace and grace of our Father
fall not on a soul in flight . . .
So if we seek peace for all people,
there is but one place to begin,
And the armament race will not win it,
for the fortress of peace is within.

Listen in Silence If You Would Hear

Silently the green leaves grow,
In silence falls the soft, white snow,
Silently the flowers bloom,
In silence sunshine fills a room—
Silently bright stars appear,
In silence velvet night draws near,
And silently God enters in
To free a troubled heart from sin . . .
For God works silently in lives.

The Peace of Meditation

So we may know God better
  and feel His quiet power,
Let us daily keep in silence
  a meditation hour . . .
For to understand God's greatness
  and to use His gifts each day,
The soul must learn to meet Him
  in a meditative way . . .
For our Father tells His children
  that if they would know His will
They must seek Him in the silence
  when all is calm and still . . .
For nature's great forces
  are found in quiet things
Like softly falling snowflakes
  drifting down on angels' wings
Or petals dropping soundlessly
  from a lovely full-blown rose—
So God comes closest to us
  when our souls are in repose . . .
So let us plan with prayerful care
  to always allocate
A certain portion of each day
  to be still and meditate . . .
For when everything is quiet
  and we're lost in meditation,
Our souls are then preparing
  for a deeper dedication
That will make it wholly possible
  to quietly endure
The violent world around us,
  for in God we are secure.

God's Keeping

To be in God's keeping
   is surely a blessing,
For, though life is often
   dark and distressing,
No day is too dark
   and no burden too great
That God in His love
   cannot penetrate.

When My Soul at Last Finds Peace

Today my soul is reaching out for something that's unknown.
I cannot grasp or fathom it, for it's known to God alone.
I cannot hold or harness it or put it into form,
For it's as uncontrollable as the wind before the storm.
I know not where it came from or whither it will go,
For it's as inexplicable as the restless winds that blow . . .
And like the wind it too will pass and leave nothing more behind
Than the memory of a mystery that blew across my mind,
But like the wind it will return to keep reminding me
That everything that has been is what again will be . . .
For there is nothing that is new beneath God's timeless sun,
And present, past, and future are all molded into one.
East and west and north and south—the same wind keeps on blowing,
While rivers run on endlessly, yet the sea's not overflowing . . .
And the restless, unknown longing of my searching soul won't cease
Until God comes in glory and my soul at last finds peace.

Learn to Rest

We all need short vacations
  in life's fast and maddening race—
An interlude of quietness
  from the constant, jet-age pace,
So when your day is pressure-packed
  and your hours are all too few,
Just close your eyes and meditate
  and let God talk to you . . .
For when we keep on pushing,
  we're not following in God's way—
We are foolish, selfish robots
  mechanized to fill each day
With unimportant trivia
  that makes life more complex
And gives us greater problems
  to irritate and vex.
So when your nervous network
  becomes a tangled mess,
Just close your eyes in silent prayer
  and ask the Lord to bless
Each thought that you are thinking,
  each decision you must make,
As well as every word you speak
  and every step you take—
For only by the grace of God
  can you gain self-control,
And only meditative thoughts
  can restore your peace of soul.

Proverbs and Wisdom

Greatness

A man may be wealthy,
Good fortune may be his fate,
But only man's motives
Can make him truly great.

Life

A little laughter, a little song,
A little teardrop
When things go wrong,
A little calm
And a little strife,
A little loving—
And that is LIFE.

Wealth

Good health, good humor,
And good sense,
No one is poor
With this defense.

Reward

If you carve your name right in a man's heart
With a kindly word and a laugh
You can be mighty sure that your tombstone
Will be carved with the right epitaph.

These four poems are from early verses in the Helen Steiner Rice Foundation archives.

The Best Things

The best things are nearest—
    breath in your nostrils,
    light in your eyes,
    flowers at your feet,
    duties at your hand,
    the path of right just before you.
Then do not grasp at the stars,
    but do life's plain, common work
    as it comes,
    certain that daily duties
    and daily bread
    are the sweetest things of life.

Remember This

Great is the power of might and mind,
But only love can make us kind,
And all we are or hope to be
Is empty pride and vanity.
If love is not a part of all,
The greatest man is very small.

Show Me the Way

Show me the way
    not to fortune and fame,
Not how to win laurels
    or praise for my name,
But show me the way
    to spread the great story
That Thine is the kingdom
    and power and glory.

A Sure Way to a Happy Day

Happiness is something we create in our minds—
It's not something you search for and so seldom find.
It's just waking up and beginning the day
By counting our blessings and kneeling to pray.
It's giving up thoughts that breed discontent
And accepting what comes as a gift heaven-sent.
It's giving up wishing for things we have not
And making the best of whatever we've got.
It's knowing that life is determined for us
And pursuing our tasks without fret, fume, or fuss . . .
For it's by completing what God gives us to do
That we find real contentment and happiness, too.

Ideals Are like Stars

In this world of casual carelessness,
    it's discouraging to try
To keep our morals and standards
    and our ideals high.
We are ridiculed and laughed at
    by the smart sophisticate,
Who proclaims in brittle banter
    that such things are out-of-date . . .
But no life is worth living
    unless it's built on truth,
And we lay our life's foundation
    in the golden years of youth . . .
So allow no one to stop you
    or hinder you from laying
A firm and strong foundation
    made of faith and love and praying . . .

And remember that ideals
    are like stars up in the sky—
You can never really reach them,
    hanging in the heavens high,
But like the mighty mariner
    who sailed the storm-tossed sea
And used the stars to chart his course
    with skill and certainty,
You too can chart your course in life
    with high ideals and love,
For high ideals are like the stars
    that light the sky above—
You cannot ever reach them,
    but lift your heart up high
And your life will be as shining
    as the stars up in the sky.

Advice for Girls

You want to be attractive and enjoy yourself while young.
You want to be admired and have your praises sung,
And all of this is natural and ordained by God above,
For God made man and woman to experience sex and love . . .
But never try to prove your love without a wedding ring,
And never deal in free love, for there is no such thing . . .
For free love is a sales pitch—it's a game you cannot win.
The best gambler is a loser when you play around with sin . . .
So do not risk your chances for a long and happy life,
A life of true fulfillment that's known only to a wife . . .
For regardless of society and the morals they disparage,
Nothing in the world can take the place of love and marriage.

Good Things for Good Business

Be cheerful, courteous, considerate,
    and cooperative at all times.
Maintain good business principles
    and an attractive business house always.
Conform to the golden rule and continue
    to profit most as you serve best.

Originally written for a 1924 business article for employers and
employees.

Meet the Success Family

Would you like an introduction
    to the family of Success?
Would you like to form a friendship
    that would lead to happiness?
Would you like to meet the father
    and the sons and daughters, too?
Would you like to know the mother
    and have the baby smile on you?
Well, meet the father—he is Work.
    The mother is Ambition.
The children are a source of pride—
    they uphold the best tradition.
The oldest son is Common Sense,
    Perseverance is his brother,
While Honesty and Foresight
    are twins to one another.
The daughter's name is Character,
    her sisters' names are Cheer
And Loyalty and Courtesy
    and Purpose That's Sincere.
The baby of the family
    is mighty sweet to know.

Its name is Opportunity—
    you'll want to see it grow.
And if you get acquainted
    with the father, you will find
The members of his family
    are just the nicest kind,
And if you form a friendship
    with the family of Success,
You'll get an introduction
    to a house of happiness.

A Prayer for the Young and Lovely

Dear God, I keep praying for the things I desire.
You tell me I'm selfish and playing with fire.
It is hard to believe I am selfish and vain—
My desires seem so real and my needs seem so sane,
And yet You are wiser and Your vision is wide,
And You look down on me and You see deep inside.
You know it's so easy to change and distort,
And things that are evil seem such harmless sport.
Oh, teach me, dear God, to not rush ahead,
But to pray for Your guidance and to trust You instead . . .
For You know what I need and that I'm only a slave
To the things that I want and desire and crave.
Oh, God, in Your mercy look down on me now
And see in my heart that I love You somehow,
Although in my rashness, impatience, and greed
I pray for the things that I want and don't need . . .
And instead of a crown, please send me a cross,
And teach me to know that all gain is but loss,
And show me the way to joy without end
With You as my Father, Redeemer, and Friend,
And send me the things that are hardest to bear,
And keep me forever safe in Thy care.

The Long View

Growing older
is like slowly going up
in an airplane.
The horizon gets wider and wider
as we look down on this earth,
and things become smaller and smaller
and of much less importance
in the panoramic view
of our soul!

Make Your Day Bright by Thinking Right

Don't start your day by supposin' that trouble is just ahead—
It's better to stop supposin' and start with a prayer instead . . .
And make it a prayer of thanksgiving for the wonderful things God has
   wrought,
Like the beautiful sunrise and sunset—God's gifts that are free and not
   bought . . .
For what is the use of supposin' that dire things could happen to you—
Worrying about some misfortune that seldom if ever comes true . . .
But instead of just idle supposin', step forward to meet each new day
Secure in the knowledge God's near you to lead you each step of the
   way . . .
For supposin' the worst things will happen only helps to make them
   come true,
And you darken the bright, happy moments that the dear Lord has
   given to you . . .
So if you desire to be happy and get rid of the misery of dread,
Just give up supposin' the worst things and look for the best things
   instead.

What Is Sin?

We ask what is sin and how does it begin.
Does it come from without or begin from within?
Well, sin is much more than an act or a deed,
More than false witness or avarice or greed,
More than adultery or killing or stealing.
Sin starts with a thought or an unworthy feeling
Long before it becomes an act, word, or deed,
For it grows deep within like a poisonous weed.
It's something we nurture and then cultivate
By conjuring up evils we then imitate,
And the longer we dwell on this evil within
The greater our urge and desire to sin
And the less our restraint of unwholesome sensations
To deny to our bodies full gratification . . .
And the more that we sin the less we detect
That in sinning we lose our own self-respect,
And slowly we sink to a still lower level
Until we become mere dupes of the devil,
For sin is so subtle, and it slips in with ease,
And it gets a firm hold where we do as we please . . .
So ask God to help you to conquer desire
Aroused by the thoughts that have set you afire,
And remember, in sinning there is no lasting joy,
For all sin can do is degrade and destroy.

Growing Older Is Part of God's Plan

You can't hold back the dawn
   or stop the tides from flowing
Or keep a rose from withering
   or still a wind that's blowing—
And time cannot be halted
   in its swift and endless flight,
For age is sure to follow youth
   like day comes after night . . .
For He who sets our span of years
   and watches from above
Replaces youth and beauty
   with peace and truth and love—
And then our souls are privileged
   to see a hidden treasure
That in youth escapes our eyes
   in our pursuit of pleasure . . .
So passing years are but blessings
   that open up the way
To the everlasting beauty
   of God's eternal day.

The Happiness You Already Have

Memories are treasures
   that time cannot destroy,
They are the happy pathway
   to yesterday's bright joy.

Heaven and Eternity

Life's Golden Autumn

Memory opens wide the door
  on a happy day like this,
And with a sweet nostalgia
  we longingly recall
The happy days of long ago
  that seem the best of all . . .
But time cannot be halted
  in its swift and endless flight,
And age is sure to follow youth
  as day comes after night,
And once again it's proven
  that the restless brain of man
Is powerless to alter
  God's great, unchanging plan . . .
But while our steps grow slower
  and we grow more tired, too,
The soul goes roaring upward
  to realms untouched and new,
Where God's children live forever
  in the beauty of His love.

Who Said, "God Is Dead"?

In this world of new concepts it has often been said—
Why heed the commandments of a God who is dead?
Why follow His precepts that are old and outdated,
Restrictive and narrow and in no way related
To this modern-day world where the pace is so fast
It cannot be hampered by an old-fashioned past . . .
And yet this "dead" God still holds in His hand
The star-studded sky, the sea, and the land,
And with perfect precision the old earth keeps spinning,
As flawlessly accurate as in the beginning . . .

So be not deceived by the new Pharisees
Who boast man has only his own self to please
And who loudly proclaim that man is a fool
Who denies himself pleasure to follow God's rule . . .
But what can they offer that will last and endure
And make life's uncertainties safe and secure?
And what, though man gain the whole world and its pleasures,
If he loses his soul and eternity's treasures?

The Great Tomorrow

There is always a tomorrow. Tomorrow belongs as
much to you as it does to me. The dawn of a new day
means the dawn of a new life. We cannot peer into its
storehouse, but the very impenetrable mystery which
enwraps the ever-approaching tomorrow is the one
thing that keeps the fires of hope constantly burning.

No matter what our yesterdays have been, tomorrow
may be different.

As long as we have life, the fires of hope will not die out;
the flame may burn low, but at the thought of a new
day, the flame which seemed dead leaps forward and
the sparks once more fly upward to spur us on.

Even if our today is filled with sadness and defeat, who
can foretell what the next day will bring to us? Let us
all eagerly await what destiny will deal us. We speak
of man meeting his fate, and we speak truthfully, for
every day we see life converged to life.

Tomorrow may hold your fate; tomorrow may mean
your victory. The great joy of expectation, the wonderment of an unknown realm, the splendor of the
vast, unlimitable future all lie in the eternal tomorrow—the day which makes life worth living.

In God's Tomorrow There Is Eternal Spring

All nature heeds the call of spring
    as God awakens everything,
And all that seemed so dead and still
    experiences a sudden thrill
As springtime lays a magic hand
    across God's vast and fertile land.
Oh, the joy in standing by
    to watch a sapphire springtime sky
Or see a fragile flower break through
    what just a day ago or two
Seemed barren ground still hard with frost,
    for in God's world, no life is lost,
And flowers sleep beneath the ground,
    but when they hear spring's waking sound,
They push themselves through layers of clay
    to reach the sunlight of God's day.
And man and woman, like flowers, too, must sleep
    until called from the darkened deep
To live in that place where angels sing
    and where there is eternal spring.

She's Living Still

Since mother went away,
    it seems she's nearer than before,
I cannot touch her hand,
    and yet she's with me more and more,
And the years have never lessened
    the longing in my heart
That came the day I realized
    that we must dwell apart,
And just as long as memory lives,
    my mother cannot die,
For in my heart she's living still
    as passing years go by.

On the Other Side of Death

Death is a gateway we all must pass through
To reach that fair land where the soul's born anew,
For man's born to die, and his sojourn on earth
Is a short span of years beginning with birth.
And like pilgrims we wander until Death takes our hand
And we start on the journey to God's Promised Land—
A place where we'll find no suffering or tears,
Where time is not counted in days, months, or years.
And in that fair city that God has prepared
Are unending joys to be happily shared
With all of our loved ones who patiently wait
On death's other side to open the gate.

I Do Not Go Alone

If Death should beckon me with outstretched hand
And whisper softly of an unknown land,
I shall not be afraid to go,
For though the path I do not know,
I take Death's hand without fear,
For He who safely brought me here
Will also take me safely back.
And though in many things I lack,
He will not let me go alone
Into the valley that's unknown . . .
So I reach out and take Death's hand
And journey to the Promised Land.

Blessings in Disguise

God sends His little angels in many forms and guises.
They come as lovely miracles that God alone devises,
For He does nothing without purpose—everything's a perfect plan
To fulfill in bounteous measure all He ever promised man . . .
For every little angel with a body bent and broken
Or a little mind challenged or little words unspoken
Is just God's way of trying to reach out and touch the hands
Of all who do not know Him and cannot understand
That often through an angel whose wings will never fly
The Lord is pointing out the way to His eternal sky,
Where there will be no handicaps of body, soul, or mind
And where all limitations will be dropped and left behind . . .
So accept these little angels as gifts from God above,
And thank Him for this lesson in faith and hope and love.

The Way of the Cross Leads to God

He carried the cross to Calvary—
Carried its burden for you and me.
There on the cross He was crucified,
And because He bled and died,
We know that whatever our cross may be,
It leads to God and eternity . . .
For who can hope for a crown of stars
Unless it is earned with suffering and scars?
For how could we face the living Lord
And rightfully claim His promised reward
If we have not carried our cross of care
And tasted the cup of bitter despair?
Let those who yearn for the pleasures of life

And long to escape all suffering and strife
Rush recklessly on to an empty goal
With never a thought of the spirit and soul—
But if you are searching to find the way
To life everlasting and eternal day,
With faith in your heart take the path that He trod,
For the way of the cross is the way to God.

I Am the Way, the Truth, and the Life

I am the Way,
    so just follow Me
Though the way be rough
    and you cannot see . . .
I am the Truth
    which all men seek,
So heed not false prophets
    nor the words that they speak . . .
I am the Life,
    and I hold the key
That opens the door
    to eternity . . .
And in this dark world,
    I am the Light
To the Promised Land
    where there is no night.

Life Is Forever! Death Is a Dream!

If we did not go to sleep at night,
We'd never awaken to see the light—
And the joy of watching a new day break
Or meeting the dawn by some quiet lake
Would never be ours unless we slept
While God and all His angels kept
A vigil through this little death
That's over with the morning's breath . . .
And death too is a time of sleeping,
For those who die are in God's keeping,
And there's a sunrise for each soul—
For life, not death, is God's promised goal . . .
So trust God's promise and doubt Him never,
For only through death can man live forever.

Because He Lives, We Too Shall Live

In this restless world of struggle
    it is very hard to find
Answers to the questions
    that daily come to mind.
We cannot see the future,
    what's beyond is still unknown,
For the secret of God's kingdom
    still belongs to Him alone.
But He granted us salvation
    when His Son was crucified,
For life became immortal
    because our Savior died.

Life Is Eternal

"Life is eternal," the good Lord said,
So do not think of your loved one as dead.
For death is only a stepping stone
To a beautiful life we have never known—
A place where God promised man he would be
Eternally happy and safe and free,
A wonderful land where we live anew
When our journey on earth is over and through.
So trust in God and doubt Him never,
For all who love Him live forever—
And while we cannot understand,
Just let the Savior take your hand,
For when death's angel comes to call,
God is so great and we are so small.
And there is nothing you need fear,
For faith in God makes all things clear.

Give Us Daily Awareness

On life's busy thoroughfares
We meet with angels unaware—
So, Father, make us kind and wise
So we may always recognize
The blessings that are ours to take,
The friendships that are ours to make
If we but open our heart's door wide
To let the sunshine of love inside—
For God is not in far distant places
But in loving hearts and friendly faces.

What Is Life?

Life is a sojourn here on earth
Which begins the day God gives us birth.
We enter this world from the great unknown,
And God gives each spirit a form of its own
And endows this form with a heart and a soul
To spur man on to his ultimate goal . . .
And through the senses of feeling and seeing,
God makes man into a human being
So he may experience a mortal life
And through this period of smiles and strife
Prepare himself to return as he came,
For birth and death are in essence the same—
For both are fashioned by God's mighty hand,
And while we cannot understand,
We know we are born to die and arise,
For beyond this world in beauty lies
The purpose of living and the ultimate goal
God gives at birth to each seeking soul . . .
So enjoy your sojourn on earth and be glad
That God gives you a choice between good things and bad,
And only be sure that you heed God's voice
Whenever life asks you to make a choice.

In God Is My Strength

"Love divine, all loves excelling,"
    make my humbled heart Your dwelling . . .
For without Your love divine,
    total darkness would be mine.
My earthly load I could not bear
    if You were not there to share
All the pain, despair, and sorrow
    that almost make me dread tomorrow,

For I am often weak and weary,
 and life is dark and bleak and dreary . . .
But somehow when I realize
 that He who made the sea and skies
And holds the whole world in His hand
 has my small soul in His command,
It gives me strength to try once more
 to somehow reach the heavenly door
Where I will live forevermore
 with friends and loved ones I adore.

Death Is a Doorway

On the wings of death the "soul takes flight"
Into the land where "there is no night,"
For those who believe what the Savior said
Will rise in glory though they be dead . . .
So death comes to us just to open the door
To the kingdom of God and life evermore.

God's Stairway

Step by step we climb day by day
Closer to God with each prayer we pray,
For the cry of the heart offered in prayer
Becomes just another spiritual stair
In the heavenly staircase leading us to
A beautiful place where we live anew . . .
So never give up, for it's worth the climb
To live forever in endless time
Where the soul of man is safe and free
To live and love through eternity.

There Is No Death

There is no night without a dawning,
    no winter without a spring,
And beyond death's dark horizon
    our hearts once more will sing.
For those who leave us for a while
    have only gone away
Out of a restless, careworn world
    into a brighter day
Where there will be no partings
    and time is not counted by years—
Where there are no trials or troubles,
    no worries, no cares, and no tears.

A World of Faith and Comfort

The waking earth in Springtime
Reminds us it is true
That nothing really ever dies
That is not born anew . . .
So trust God's all wise wisdom
And doubt the Father never,
For in His Heavenly Kingdom
There is nothing lost forever.

The Home Beyond

We feel so sad when those we love
Are called to live in the home above,
But why should we grieve when they say good-bye
And go to dwell in a cloudless sky?
For they have but gone to prepare the way,
And we'll meet them again some happy day,

For God has told us that nothing can sever
A life He created to live forever.
So let God's promise soften our sorrow
And give us new strength for a brighter tomorrow.

Death Opens the Door to Life Evermore

We live a short while on earth below,
Reluctant to die, for we do not know
Just what dark death is all about,
And so we view it with fear and doubt.
Not certain of what is around the bend,
We look on death as the final end
To all that made us mortal beings,
And yet there lies beyond our seeing
A beautiful life so full and complete
That we should leave with hurrying feet
To walk with God by sacred streams
Amid beauty and peace beyond our dreams,
For all who believe in the risen Lord
Have been assured of this reward,
And death for them is just graduation
To a higher realm of wide elevation.
For life on earth is a transient affair—
Just a few brief years in which to prepare
For a life that is free from pain and tears,
Where time is not counted by hours or years.
For death is only the method God chose
To colonize heaven with the souls of those
Who by their apprenticeship on earth
Proved worthy to dwell in the land of new birth.
So death is not sad—it's a time for elation,
A joyous transition, the soul's emigration
Into a place where the soul's safe and free
To live with God through eternity.

God's Messengers

The unexpected kindness
    from an unexpected place,
A hand outstretched in friendship,
    a smile on someone's face,
A word of understanding
    spoken in a time of trial
Are unexpected miracles
    that make life more worthwhile.
We know not how it happened
    that in an hour of need
Somebody out of nowhere
    proved to be a friend indeed . . .
For God has many messengers
    we fail to recognize,
But He sends them when we need them,
    and His ways are wondrous and wise . . .
So keep looking for an angel
    and keep listening to hear,
For on life's busy, crowded streets,
    you will find God's presence near.

When I Must Leave You

When I must leave you for a little while,
Please go on bravely with a gallant smile
And for my sake and in my name,
Live on and do all things the same—
Spend not your life in empty days,
But fill each waking hour in useful ways—
Reach out your hand in comfort and in cheer,
And I in turn will comfort you and hold you near.

Yesterday, Today, and Tomorrow

Yesterday's dead, tomorrow's unborn,
So there's nothing to fear and nothing to mourn,
For all that is past and all that has been
Can never return to be lived once again . . .
And what lies ahead or the things that will be
Are still in God's hands, so it is not up to me
To live in the future that is God's great unknown,
For the past and the present God claims for His own . . .
So all I need do is to live for today
And trust God to show me the truth and the way,
For it's only the memory of things that have been
And expecting tomorrow to bring trouble again
That fills my today, which God wants to bless,
With uncertain fears and borrowed distress . . .
For all I need live for is this one little minute,
For life's here and now and eternity's in it.

Death Is the Gateway to Eternal Life

Death is just another step along life's changing way—
No more than just a gateway to a new and better day—
And parting from our loved ones is much easier to bear
When we know that they are waiting for us to join them there . . .
For it is on the wings of death that the living soul takes flight
Into the Promised Land of God where there shall be no night . . .
So death is just a natural thing, like the closing of a door
As we start upon a journey to a new and distant shore . . .
And none need make this journey undirected or alone,
For God promised us safe passage to this vast and great unknown . . .
So let your grief be softened and yield not to despair—
You have only placed your loved one in the loving Father's care.

Our Father Will Provide

Death is a gateway our loved ones pass through
On their way to a land where we're all born anew,
And while we can't see what's on death's other side,
We know that our Father will richly provide
All that He promised to those who believe,
And His kingdom is waiting for us to receive.

About the End

And now that you've come to the end of this book,
Pause and reflect and take a swift backward look
And you'll find that to follow God's commandment each day
Is not only the righteous and straight, narrow way
But a joyous experience, for there's many a thrill
In going God's way and in doing His will . . .
For in traveling God's way you are never alone,
For all of your problems God takes as His own,
And always He's ready to counsel and guide you,
And in sadness or gladness He's always beside you . . .
And to live for God's glory and to walk in His truth
Brings peace to the angel and joy to the youth,
And at the end of life's journey, there's His promised reward
Of life everlasting in the house of the Lord.

With His Love

If you found any beauty in the poems in this book
    or some peace and comfort in a word or a line,
Don't give me the praise or the worldly acclaim,
    for the words that you read are not mine.
I borrowed them all to share with you
    from our heavenly Father above,
And the joy that you felt was God speaking to you
    as he flooded your heart with His love.

Index of Titles

Index of First Lines

Helen Steiner Rice Foundation

Whatever the celebration, whatever the day, whatever the event, whatever the occasion, Helen Steiner Rice possessed the ability to express the appropriate feeling for that particular moment. A happening became happier, a sentiment more sentimental, a memory more memorable because of her deep sensitivity and ability to put into understandable language the emotion being experienced. Her positive attitude, her concern for others, and her love of God are identifiable threads woven into her life, her work . . . and even her death.

Prior to Mrs. Rice's passing, she established the Helen Steiner Rice Foundation, a nonprofit corporation that awards grants to worthy charitable programs assisting the elderly and the needy.

Royalties from the sale of this book will add to the financial capabilities of the Helen Steiner Rice Foundation. Because of limited resources, the foundation presently limits grants to qualified charitable programs in Lorain, Ohio, where Helen Steiner Rice was born, and Greater Cincinnati, Ohio, where Mrs. Rice lived and worked most of her life. Hopefully in the future, resources will be of sufficient size that broader geographical areas may be considered in the awarding of grants.

Because of her foresight, caring, and deep conviction of sharing, Helen Steiner Rice continues to touch a countless number of lives through foundational grants and through her inspirational poetry. Thank you for your assistance in helping to keep Helen's dream alive and growing.

Andrea R. Cornett, Administrator